Seasons on the Severn

Kelvin Worthington

Published by New Generation Publishing in 2022

First Edition

ISBN   978-1-80369-480-1

www.newgeneration-publishing.com

New Generation Publishing

There are many people to thank for their contributions to this book, not least the fishing friends whom I have had the pleasure to spend many happy hours with at riverside and lakeside. Many thanks also to Nick Fisher for his foreword and for all his support of this venture. Last, but by no means least, especial gratitude and thanks to my wonderful wife, Helen, for her unstinting support and encouragement of my various endeavours.

Contents

Foreword

One of the most intangible and frustrating things about fishing - apart from not being able to catch anything - is explaining exactly what fishing is. Fishing is so many different things to so many people. It's wild seas and huge pelagic beasts, it's teeny tiny flies and ruby spotted trout, it's wide raging rivers or still silent canals. Fishing is a very broad church indeed.

And yet, what Kelvin does so well in this delightful book is to identify so succinctly what fishing means to him and exactly where it lives in his life and his heart.

All of us who go fishing regularly feel it tug on our emotions or tease at our conscious and unconscious thoughts. It's this that compels and propels us to go fishing again and again. Even if we don't exactly understand why. Why we don't just go and play golf or stay in the garage to wax some already obscenely shiny classic car. Why we instead choose to go out in the world of Nature where we have little or no control of our day's outcome. And why we can still derive pleasure, reward and even encouragement from a totally fish-less day.

Fishing fills some inexplicable void that nothing else even touches. It's as though anglers have some mysterious gland that is stimulated by the prospect or the memory of a day around water. Kelvin's writing shows so clearly that he is a brother of the angle, that he hears the beat of that drum, that pulse, that watery siren call.

I used to sit at my desk in Carnaby Street, Central London, writing features for a teenage music and fashion magazine, while secretly I day-dreamed of sea trout. I had a box of flies hidden in my desk drawer beside my 80's Filofax and Sony Walkman. A box of sea trout flies, that I would sneakily peek into during the day, the sight of those creations of feather and fur transporting me to a happy water-filled place, far away from the world of Boy George and leg warmers.

Kelvin's happy place is the River Severn, which has flowed through his veins and drenched his memory cells since he was knee high. To share Kelvin's love of angling and to feel the enthusiasm and joy it has brought him and *still* brings him, through his writing, is a delight.

To Kelvin fishing is a thing of wellness, mindfulness, mediation and memories linked together into a beautiful thread that winds through the fabric of his years making him a more whole, more happy, more contented person.

And I have to say, reading about his adventures makes me one too.

Nick Fisher

Creator and writer of Screaming Reels, Dirty Tackle and The River Cottage Book of Fish.

About the Author

The countryside has always been a great passion of Kelvin Worthington. From an early age he was a member of the Royal Society for the Protection of Birds and from the age of about eight also became hooked on fishing.

In his youth he lived on a farm and got to know the local gamekeeper. In doing so he became involved in the pastime of rough shooting and also assisted as a beater on the local syndicate shoot.

So, the countryside is in his blood and, as like-minded folk will tell you, you can take the person out of the countryside, but you can't take the countryside out of the person!

Born in a Shropshire village located near to the River Severn, the river, its fishing, its countryside and its history has featured strongly throughout Kelvin's life from an early age. From early casts for perch, barbel and chub (without too much success, as you will read) at Ironbridge and Jackfield, to adulthood fishing for barbel and chub (with marginally more success) at Buildwas, Atcham and Bewdley, the river has always been a place of peace and retreat, away from the stresses of work and modern life.

Kelvin worked for Barclays Bank for 25 years, latterly as a corporate banking manager based in Shrewsbury, which, perhaps not surprisingly, is also on the Severn. His role covered a large geographical area within Shropshire – a county through which the Severn flows a great deal. Therefore, he has never been far away from the river and the countryside.

Kelvin is a published author on the subjects of business, finance, setting up and running a small business, accounting, and personal finance, but has always had the desire to write a book about the river which has featured so much in his life, and which has bought him so much pleasure over the years. This is that book. We hope you enjoy it.

Preface

As a child and teenager I was raised on the wonderfully evocative and pioneering fishing and countryside television programmes of Jack Hargreaves ("Old Country") and John Wilson ("Go Fishing"). I have also long been an admirer of the writings of Chris Yates and, especially, 'BB', having a large collection of books written by both authors, together with other wonderful works such as those of H T Sheringham, Howard Marshall, Jack Hargreaves, Bernard Venables, John Wilson and John Bailey. BB's book "A Summer on the Nene" is especially inspirational in the desire to write this book.

Whilst I would never claim to be in the same league as the afore-mentioned, both as a fisherman or a writer, I intend to attempt (in my own inadequate way) to capture some of the beauty and majesty of the River Severn – the longest in the British Isles – its wildlife, its fish and the changing moods of the river and its surrounding countryside throughout the seasons.

The River Severn has its innocuous birth in the moorlands of Central Wales, from whence it embarks upon a seeming life journey, through its bubbling adolescence as it crosses the border into England, then onwards through its melancholy mid-life as it meanders past historic towns such as Shrewsbury and Worcester, including a brief mid-life crisis as it tumbles over the rapids of the Ironbridge Gorge, before finally ending its life as it throws itself into the Irish Sea at Bristol.

As a boy I fished the river, as a complete novice and hopeless angler, at Ironbridge. After an extended period away from both fishing and the river, I returned as an adult to once more fish its powerful wides as it meanders its way past Buildwas.

I recall many happy early mornings in summer, walking across the fields to the river, not able to see it for the early morning mist and strange half-light, but hearing its call as it chortled and chuckled over the shallows. My only companions were the cows in the fields, which materialized through the mist like ghosts, singularly uninterested in me or my purpose, just intent on eating the lush green grass with its covering of early morning dew.

The Severn has featured in a large part of my life and has blessed me with many happy memories, so it feels appropriate to try to repay that gift by writing what I hope will be a fitting tribute to the river and its journey through the beautiful and varied countryside and surroundings which are inextricably linked to the very life of the river itself.

I have chosen the title Seasons on the Severn to essentially reflect the natural seasons, however this book, in a sense, also reflects the seasons of my life from childhood through to early and later adulthood. Throughout these life seasons, my beloved River Severn has been my companion and my joy, and I look forward to returning to it soon, perhaps in the next season of my life, to enjoy its company, its wildlife and its fishing once again.

It is my fervent hope that this book brings you as much pleasure reading it as it has to me in writing it, and that it will perhaps encourage you to make a trip to the Severn, to enjoy its heritage, countryside, wildlife and, not least, its excellent fishing.

Kelvin Worthington

Chapter 1 – My First Fishing Trip

~~~~~~~~~

I must have been aged about eight when I went on my first fishing trip on the River Severn.

A neighbour of ours who ran a small market garden also owned a field near Newtown in Wales. The Severn ran through the field and the neighbour, as owner, enjoyed the fishing rights on that small stretch of the river. He had bought an old caravan and left it parked in the field so that he could spend a weekend, when his business allowed, fishing for river trout which were plentiful in those upper reaches of the river.

One Saturday morning in early Summer our neighbour, my father, my older brother, and I piled into our neighbour's car, and we set off on the two-hour journey to the field which our neighbour owned. Whilst I use the word 'car' it was actually a small Morris pick-up, with a cab up front and an open flat load space behind, which was used to take fruit and vegetables to market. This space, usually occupied by fruit and vegetables, was currently filled with our fishing tackle including my first proper rod which I had been given for my recent birthday. It was a glass-fibre 2-piece rod of about 10 ½ feet and was sandy yellow in colour. In those days glass-fibre rods were the affordable way of going fishing as carbon rods were just coming in and were still very expensive.

In the front of the car, we all sat in a row across the bench-type seat, as there were no rear seats. Being the smallest I was broadly in the middle, with one leg either side of the long spindly gear stick which protruded from the floor somewhere under the dashboard in front of me. I was instructed to be very careful not to knock the gearstick with my legs and, taking this instruction very seriously, sat like a rock throughout the whole journey. Needless to say, I was very thankful when we arrived at our destination, and I was able to stretch my legs and breathe again.

The field owned by our neighbour was given over to grass, and a number of sheep were contentedly cropping the green swards. They were the typical hardy Welsh variety and were owned by the local farmer who had some sort of arrangement with our neighbour to allow grazing, I think in return for keeping an eye on our neighbour's old caravan to ensure that no one ran off with it. The river ran along the far side of the field, being flanked by stunted birch trees, typical of those found in large areas of mid and north Wales.

It was by now mid-morning and the sun was high in the sky and shining brightly. There was hardly a breath of wind, and the river was crystal clear – hardly the best conditions for catching wily brown trout. I tackled up with 3lb line straight through to a size 10 hook with a lobworm for bait. My float was a lovely old crow-quill which was about eight inches long with an attractive orange painted tip. It was fixed top and bottom by float rubbers, about three feet above the hook. A small number of dust shot, spaced out shirt-button style to allow a natural drop through the water completed my rig. I felt that I wouldn't need any heavier shot because the current on this stretch was very leisurely and I was sure that the weight of the lobworm itself would take it down to the waiting trout.

I sat on the riverbank nearly dangling my feet in the water and cast underarm into the middle of the river, which was about 50 feet wide at this point. The lovely orange tip of the float showed up beautifully and I watched as it sailed off downstream to where I hoped the trout would be waiting for their lunch. In fact, I knew they were there because I could see them. The river was so clear and calm that it was easy to see through the surface of the water to where little shapes wavered in the current, occasionally veering sideways across the river to intercept a passing morsel.

I was tremendously excited by all this, especially with today being my first proper fishing trip, and I felt sure that very soon one of those little shapes would grab my worm and I would have caught my first fish. Unfortunately, looking back I can see that I had at that time not learnt the first rule of angling – the art of concealment. In my excitement I kept standing up to better see my float, which was by this time approximately 25 yards downstream and, of course, as soon as I did this, I spooked the trout, and they would not come near my juicy worm. Time and time again I reeled in and recast, letting my float travel downstream until I could barely see it in the distance, and each time the trout steadfastly refused to have a nibble.

Somewhat frustrated I paused fishing to have some lunch, consisting of a cheese sandwich and a bag of crisps, washed down with a bottle of pop. Being out in that lovely open countryside seemed to add additional flavour to my lunch and even now I can recall it being one of the best picnics I ever had. The sun was warm on my face and as I lay back in the grass, I could see buzzards circling overhead, riding invisible waves of warm air currents with consummate ease, their mewing gull-like 'pee-oo' call mixing with the bleating of the sheep and the chuckling of the river into one harmonious symphony. Occasionally, in the distance, I could also hear the plaintive call of the curlew and the soaringly beautiful song of the skylark, both so evocative of these sparsely inhabited hills and river valleys.

Lulled by so much beauty, I think I must have dozed off for a little while, during which my brother tried to get 'one up' on me by catching a fish, thankfully unsuccessfully. With renewed vigour I retackled and made my way to the riverside.

This time I decided to be sneaky and instead of using a worm as bait, I was using the crusts of my sandwiches which I had kept from my lunch. As I wasn't keen on the crusts anyway, it wasn't too much of a sacrifice. I broke the crusts up into small pieces the size of my little fingernail and threw some of them into the water to float down to the waiting fish, who I hoped were now ready for their lunch too. I then put another small piece on my hook.

As the pieces of crust which I had thrown in floated downstream they were intercepted with great delight by the trout and I, feeling very pleased with my little deception, felt sure that it would only be a matter of time before my hook bait was taken too. Regretfully the trout seemed to know which piece of bread had my hook in it, and they continued over the next couple of hours to steadfastly ignore that piece in favour of the pieces without a hook inside.

Afternoon ran into evening, and it was time to go home. We packed away our tackle in the back of the pick-up, climbed wearily into the front and set off. It must have been all that fresh air, or exhaustion caused by the frustrating trout, but I slept most of the way home. At least I didn't then have to think about keeping absolutely still so as not to knock the gear stick.

Despite not having caught a fish – in fact none of us did – it was still a wonderful day. Spending time at the riverside in such beautiful surroundings, observing nature all around you, is one of the most profitable ways of spending your time – a sentiment that many anglers will know and agree with. Angling takes you to beautiful places many people never get to experience, and brings you closer to the wonders of nature, allowing you time to take stock of life and recharge your batteries for the days ahead.

Anglers are indeed the most privileged of people.

~~~~~~~~~~

Chapter 2 – Lessons Learned

~~~~~~~~~~

Approximately 2 miles downstream from the village of Ironbridge is the site of a riverside pub called "The Half Moon". The pub, at the time, was an old black and white timber-framed building, although a new, more modern pub now sits on the site, which has a wide frontage to the river.

The pub itself is set back approximately 30 yards from the river, and its lawns slope down to the waterside, so it was (and still is) a very popular place on summer evenings for people to sit on the grass whilst having a drink.

The pub is also known to me for the reason that the brass band I was a member of used to hold summer evening concerts on the pub lawns, and this was also one of the regular places where I used to play "The Last Post" as part of Remembrance Sunday events.

I remember many cold, still, frosty November mornings at this spot, trying to warm my lips enough to be able to play my cornet and attempting to stop my hands from freezing to the cornet's metal, whilst at the same time marvelling at the beauty of the surroundings all covered in frost. In some years the grass and trees were white over with Jack Frost's icy touch, and cobwebs hung gently in the hedgerows, highly visible in their silvery coating of frost. Interestingly, when there was a hard frost and the trees, grass and hedgerows were a pure white colour, the river always seemed to be a dark grey-black colour as it flowed through this otherwise pristine landscape. Somehow the purity of the white frost seemed to highlight the darker side of the river's colour, whereas at other times of the year the colour of the river blends more seamlessly into its surroundings.

It was at this spot where, as a boy aged about 10, I learned two very important lessons early in my fishing life...........

As I mentioned earlier, the pub's lawns sloped gently down to the river and these were a favourite spot for folk to have a drink and maybe even a picnic on a warm summer evening. More importantly to me and my older brother the pub had the rights to the fishing along that stretch of the river and an evening ticket was just a few pence, making it a very affordable spot for young boys to spend their paper round money on a warm summer's evening. Our parents also thought it was a good spot for us to go fishing, because there were always plenty of people around, but in the event that one of us did fall into the river our father didn't have far to run from the bar to save us.

The river in front of the pub is probably 50 yards wide and starts as a strong deep run which then shallows up into a long set of very strong rapids, which would do justice to a white-water rafting course. The evening in question was slightly overcast, warm and sultry, just right for barbel and chub fishing. The house martins which nested under the eaves of the pub, and also in the various outbuildings, were hawking across the river catching flies with gusto. Damselflies were in abundance too, alighting their slender blue bodies onto the riverside vegetation. Gnats were also in abundance, and less pleasant to encounter, but that just added to the overall atmosphere.

My brother and I started fishing in the deeper water above the rapids. I was particularly fascinated by the way the river gathered pace as it approached the rapids and then threw itself into the white water below. I was sure that this deeper water just above the rapids contained huge numbers of fish and, therefore, with a bottle of Vimto in hand for sustenance, I set up my tackle.

As I have alluded to, I was at this stage a young boy, but I was also a very inexperienced fisherman. I had read some books on fishing, but my natural impatience meant that I invariably completely ignored the good advice they gave and just did my own thing.

I set up my rod, which was a 10 ½ foot glass fibre rod and sandy yellow in colour (weren't they all?) and to this I attached a fixed spool reel loaded with 10lb breaking strain line. As a young boy I was convinced that I was going to catch a monster every time I went fishing and therefore didn't want to lose it by fishing too light. The fact that my 10lb line must have been as thick as rope probably explains why I didn't catch many fish, as my quarry must have been able to see it from a mile away.

To the line I attached a huge green and orange bodied waggler float (not because it was the best float for the conditions but because I liked the look of it) a size 10 hook (again with the monster in mind) and 4 BB shot. Bait was 4 maggots hooked quite well really - I had at least remembered what one book had told me about gently pinching the maggot and just nicking the hook into the broad end, without bursting the maggot itself.

Once in the river the float looked great and I felt very proud of myself, with all those people watching from the pub lawns. Despite the 4 BB shot the float stood up out of the water like a lighthouse, and certainly you could see it from as far away as you can a lighthouse. Despite this, the float trotted through really smoothly and, just before the point where the steady flow turned into bubbling rapids, it slid under, and I struck. The float came whizzing out of the water, nearly blinding me and just missing the courting couple on the bank behind me, who were not impressed and quickly found somewhere else to do their courting.

Unperturbed, I checked my bait, which was still fine, and recast. At exactly the same spot the float went under again. This time I struck more gently but missed the bite. However, suitably encouraged I checked my bait and cast again. After an hour of getting bites in exactly the same place every cast, but without contacting a fish, I was getting very frustrated and decided that this float fishing lark was no good and that I would change to ledger tactics and also move to the rapids, where no doubt the fish would be more accommodating.

Looking back years later I realized that what was happening was that as the water shallowed up above the rapids my float was set too deep and was dragging on the bottom, pulling the float under every time. Lesson number one learned – plumb the depth of your entire swim before fishing.

Moving slightly downstream to the faster water of the rapids, I became caught up in the excitement of the churning, bubbling water and got quite excited myself. Surely here lay the monster which I was destined to catch?

Because of the lower summer water level, a long pebbly beach had become exposed and so I climbed down the small bank and settled myself down on the pebbles, right at the water's edge. I put a drilled bullet, which I thought would roll down the swim, onto my line and stopped it about 18 inches from the size 10 hook with a BB shot. I decided to also change baits and this time put a large lump of luncheon meat onto the hook, as I had remembered from my fishing books that barbel and chub love luncheon meat.

I cast into the fast water and the bait quickly swung down and around, coming to rest in some slack water just on the edge of the rapids, and close into my own bank.

At that point I don't know if it was the excitement or the bottle of Vimto I had consumed earlier, but I desperately needed to answer the call of nature, so, putting my rod down on the pebbles I climbed back up the bank and into the bushes where no-one from the pub could see me.

A number of anglers have long held the theory that fish, wily characters that they are, wait until you are not concentrating on catching them and then at that precise moment grab your bait. Sure enough, as I was in the middle of my business in the bushes, my rod suddenly careered around and started bouncing off down the pebbly beach, being dragged, no doubt, by the monster.

I don't know what the patrons of the pub made of it, but they were suddenly treated to the sight of a young boy bursting out of the bushes, desperately trying to do up his trouser zip, then leaping over the pebbles trying to catch his fishing rod, which seemed to have a mind of its own and was on its way to Bridgnorth, some 10 miles downstream.

Fortunately, as a boy I was quite fast over short distances and managed to grab my rod before it actually got to Bridgnorth. As I picked it up, I could feel something pulling hard, but with 10lb line to fight against, the fish obviously realized it was a foregone conclusion and came relatively quietly up through the fast water, and I was able to ease it gently onto the pebbles at my feet, having left behind my landing net higher up the bank in the desperate rush to catch my fast-disappearing rod.

It was a lovely brassy chub of about 2lbs and was, at that time, not only my first chub but also my biggest ever fish. To me it was certainly the monster I had been trying to catch. It was hooked just inside the lip, and I quickly unhooked it, sliding it back into the water where it soon disappeared from view.

I was so pleased and excited that I had another bottle of Vimto to celebrate.

But another important lesson had been learned – never leave your rod unattended with the hook bait in the water.

~~~~~~~~~~

Chapter 3 – Perch in the Shadow of the Iron Bridge

~~~~~~~~~~

As the Severn enters what is known as the Ironbridge Gorge, the valley sides become steeper and start to crowd in on the river. Any houses built along here cling precariously to the steep hillsides. The light seems to fade slightly due to the lack of sunlight, which is blocked out by the high sides of the gorge. The western side of the gorge is heavily wooded, but the eastern side has many houses, which run along to the small town of Ironbridge, where the famous Iron Bridge majestically spans the river.

The bridge was the first in the world to be made from iron, and was cast locally at Coalbrookdale in the foundries of Abraham Darby III, the grandson of the first Abraham Darby. Darby started constructing the bridge in 1777, completing it in 1779. The techniques used in the construction were adapted from the well-established wood-working methods of the time, except that instead of wooden pegs holding the joints together iron ones were used. The bridge is a masterpiece of construction for its time and still sits proudly, with excellent views upstream and downstream from its mid-way point, where a cast iron centrepiece announces its construction date.

This whole area is a UNESCO-designated World Heritage Site due to it being acknowledged as the birthplace of the Industrial Revolution. This title comes about from the fact that in this area, in 1709, Abraham Darby first devised a method for smelting iron using coke instead of charcoal. For the first time it was possible to smelt iron on a mass-produced scale, thereby reducing the cost and thus making iron significantly more accessible than before. The rest, as they say, is history. It is hard to imagine what this area must have looked like at that time, but the Ironbridge Gorge Museum provides an insight to this. The museum houses paintings of the time, depicting the valley sides starkly outlined against the red fire of the many blast furnaces operating in the area. It almost looks like a scene depicting Hades itself, and was certainly a time of great hardship for those working in such conditions.

The river had a major role to play in the development of this area as an industrial powerhouse, transporting iron and china (for the gorge was also famous for its china production) downstream to Bristol, from where it was exported around the World. Boats, or as they are more correctly known, barges plied their way along the river and the whole area must have been a seething mass of activity in its heyday. Today the river is much quieter, running strongly and deeply along the bottom of the gorge, with occasional sections of strong rapids.

At one end of the Iron Bridge is a Tourist Information Centre and at the other end is a hotel called the Tontine Inn. When my mother was young, she recalls that it was possible to stand where the Information Centre now is and look across the bridge straight into the front door of the Tontine Inn. Nowadays, however, the bridge has a pronounced peak in the middle which obscures this view. Years of subsidence of the sides of the gorge have gradually squeezed the bridge, causing the centre to rise significantly. There is ongoing work to arrest this subsidence, which is a common feature of this whole stretch of the gorge until the land flattens out beyond Apley, some 5 miles downstream.

On the eastern bank of the river, where the Iron Bridge spans the gorge, is the little market square of Ironbridge itself. When I was young this was a busy place with a Lloyds Bank and other important shops where the locals did their shopping – long before the nearby new town of Telford was built, with its mega shopping centre and supermarkets. These days, the majority of folk quietly wandering around the square are tourists, but this still provides trade for the various shops, including a butcher's shop which sells the best pork pies! Above the square, perched up on the hillside, is the lovely church of St Luke which seems to watch benevolently over the square, the bridge and the river below.

Looking downstream from the bridge it is possible to see a large building away in the distance, high up on the eastern side of the gorge. This was once the residence of the afore-mentioned Abraham Darby, from where he could survey all that was going on down in the gorge below. He would have been able to see the many furnaces burning away all day and night and the multitude of barges plying their way up and down the river. Nowadays the property is an hotel, but it is still worth a visit to stand in the grounds and look down into the gorge, imagining the view as Abraham Darby might have seen it over 200 years previously.

Just downstream of the Iron Bridge, on the eastern bank, there is a row of small, terraced houses. In one of these lived the Rogers family. Probably the most well-known member of the family was Eustace Rogers, who was known to my mother (and subsequently to me) as the coracle man. Mr Rogers used to make coracles, the traditional craft of folk making their living on the river. Originally made out of animal skin stretched over a wooden frame and waterproofed with tar, these small oval craft are highly manoeuvrable in the right hands, and were popular with local fisherman who used them to set their nets to catch the eels and salmon which made their way up and down the river.

Across the river from the row of cottages where the Rogers family lived, on the western bank, is a pair of riverside cottages which are very familiar to me. One of them was owned by the aunt of a school mate of mine, Glen. What was most interesting to us as schoolboy fishermen was that Glen's aunt's cottage had a small landing stage on the river, which was an ideal place from which to fish for perch.

Most schoolboys who go fishing at some time catch perch, even if this lovely fish is not the intended prey. The reason for this is that perch love worms, bait much used by schoolboys because they are easy to obtain (by digging up father's garden) and keep well if put in a container with damp moss or soggy newspaper. Worms also do not need to be kept in the fridge like maggots do, therefore being much preferred to the latter by mothers who seem to have a problem with maggots being kept in fridges along with food for the family.

In modern terms perch could be described as fish with attitude. If you are ever fortunate enough to see a perch holding station near a bait, with its spiky dorsal fin erect and beautiful blood-red fins quivering in the invisible currents of the water you will understand what I mean. Add to these features a camouflage outfit of green and grey with tiger-like stripes down its side and you have an ideal predator.

On this particular day in summer, Glen and I arrived at his aunt's house at about 9 o'clock in the morning, having cycled there from our homes approximately 5 miles away. After quickly saying hello to her we hurried down to the little wooden landing stage and excitedly started to tackle up. We had come prepared for a long session, with cheese sandwiches for lunch, bags of crisps and bottles of fizzy orange pop (because it was school summer holidays, and the weather was reasonably warm). The river was fining down after rain the previous week, was nicely coloured and these conditions, combined with the slightly overcast sky, made us feel sure that we would have a good day.

The landing stage was only about 12 inches above the water level, so we really felt like we were floating on the water itself, as our eye line was so near to the water level. About 50 yards upstream the 200-year-old Iron Bridge towered over us, and people looked down from it to see what we were up to.

The cottage next door to the aunt's cottage also had a wooden landing stage, which was about 10 yards upstream of us. The two landing stages had a little bay between them, a small backwater where the water rested before swirling back out into the main flow and continuing its journey downstream. The water entered this little backwater at the downstream end then circled back upstream before re-joining the river. The land between the two landing stages was in the form of a high bank, covered in thick brambles which overhung the water below - an ideal spot for perch, or so we hoped.

Because the little bay was only big enough for one of us to fish in, we decided to take it in turns to fish there for perch. Whoever was not fishing the bay would fish the river itself for chub or, if we were really lucky, perhaps even a barbel. We tossed a coin, which nearly fell in the river, and Glen won so he got to fish the bay first. In the meantime, I set up to ledger fish the river using my 10 ½ foot glass fibre rod and fixed spool reel loaded with 10lb line, which was probably far too heavy a breaking strain for the conditions but my abject fear of losing a big fish because of the line breaking meant that I tended to over-compensate.

The ledger weight was a reasonably sized drilled bullet because the river at this point is squeezed by the sharply rising valley sides and runs strong and deep. Therefore, I needed quite a heavy ledger if I was to hold bottom. Bait was a big juicy worm on a size 10 hook.

Glen was using an 11-foot glass fibre rod, with 6lb line on a fixed spool reel. The float he was using was a proper perch float, about 4 inches long with a lovely bulbous body on a slender stem, topped with an attractive orange tip and fixed top and bottom with float rubbers. He selected a large worm and hooked it through the middle with a size 10 hook. We weren't too concerned about using larger worms because perch have enormous mouths and can swallow prey much bigger than one would imagine.

With both of us now ready to start fishing I cast into the middle of the river and allowed the current to swing the bait around towards my bank, downstream of our position. Once the ledger had settled, I put the rod in a rod rest and concentrated on the tip so that I could see any bites. I had the rod tip quite high in the air so that it was silhouetted against the sky, making it easier to see. As the town square of Ironbridge, with its shops and other buildings, was immediately across the river from our position it was difficult to see the tip when this was the background. Raising the rod tip a little bit higher, so that it was viewed against the sky, solved the problem.

Meanwhile Glen had swung his float out into the small bay using an underhand cast and the current immediately started to take it slowly up the backwater in an upstream direction, tantalisingly working along close to the bank of dense bushes and undergrowth. The little perch float looked absolutely splendid, with the orange tip easily visible against the darker colouring of the water. I was so completely absorbed in watching the tip of my rod that I didn't hear Glen's exclamation when his float dipped under, and he was into a fish. His rod tip bounced as the fish tried to take him into the branches of the bushes which reached down into the water, but Glen's stout tackle won the day and after a brief fight a perch of about half a pound came flapping over the edge of the landing net and into the mesh.

Even though the fish was not huge and the line was strong enough to swing the fish to hand Glen and I didn't like doing this for fear of damaging the fish's mouth, so we always used a landing net for anything weighing more than a couple of ounces. We put the net down on a small patch of grass to protect the fish from lying on any stones and gravel and had a good look at our prize. The perch positively bristled with attitude and was a glorious green with black tiger stripes and red fins. Quickly unhooking it we slipped it back into the water and it immediately dashed off to the cover of the submerged bushes, no doubt to sulk about being caught.

The deal Glen and I had negotiated with each other was that once one of us had caught a fish we would swap positions and use each other's rod, so that we both had a go at fishing for the perch, which were our main quarry of the day. So, I moved onto Glen's rod, and he took up position at my rod, which was still showing no signs of activity. Perhaps there weren't any chub or barbel in this section of the river?

I re-baited Glen's hook with another worm and excitedly swung the bait out into the little backwater. As before, the float took the bait slowly upstream, hugging the overhanging bushes on my left. About halfway up the backwater the float perceptibly slowed and shuddered slightly, sending little rings outwards across the surface of the river. As any angler will know, this first contact with something down in the depths of the river or lake is like an electric shock which comes all the way up the line and down the rod to where your hand is now tightly gripping the handle. My heart rate went up a few notches and I resisted, with difficulty, the almost overwhelming urge to strike because perch need time to inspect the bait before they take it properly.

The float shuddered again, this time a bit more strongly and dipped slightly in the water. Grinding my teeth with a mixture of excitement and nervousness I again resisted the temptation to strike. At last, the float slid away as the perch, with a firm hold on my worm, set off for his lair under the bushes. I struck gently and immediately felt the contact with this living, jerking thing on the end of my line. It felt a good fish and I had to apply a fair amount of side strain to keep him out of the bushes. The rod bent over nicely and using a combination of the line and the cushioning effect of the rod I encouraged the perch out into the open water. Once there it was a relatively easy thing to bring him up to the surface and to slide the landing net under him.

My prize was a beautiful perch of about a pound, which lay on the grass with the worm still visible, wriggling in the corner of the perch's mouth. I slipped the hook out and lifted the perch up slightly to have a better look at him, taking care not to lift him too high off the ground, just in case I dropped him and caused him harm. As I admired my catch it made me think that perch really are an archetypal predator, with large eyes for seeing their prey in dim light conditions, and marvellous camouflage colouring to assist them in ambushing their prey.

Not wanting to keep the fish out of the water for too long I knelt down and gently lowered him into the water. With a brisk swish of his tail, he shot off down into the depths and was gone from sight.

Glen and I continued to swap rods each time one of us caught something and we spent a super day catching more perch from that little backwater together with a nice little roach which also fancied one of our worms.

We never did catch anything on the ledger rod but that did not bother us too much as the perch were our main quarry that day and we caught a good enough number to keep two young boys very happy as we cycled home in the late afternoon, arriving home just in time for tea.

~~~~~~~~~~

Chapter 4 – Barbel by the Band Hut

~~~~~~~~~~

Downstream from the town of Iron Bridge the valley sides become steeper and the river enters a phase of long steady glides punctuated by a series of very strong sets of rapids. The rapids have vicious currents which even the strongest swimmer would find difficult to counter. In fact, I recall a teenage boy from the year below me at school sadly drowning at this very place one summer. Despite the beautiful surroundings of the river and its oft apparent serenity, it can still be a place of great danger to those who do not give it the respect it deserves.

Along this stretch of the river, on the eastern bank, used to be the offices and workshops of Elcock's Coaches (now called Elcock Reisen and based in nearby Madeley), which operated the school buses that I caught each day from home in Broseley to school in Much Wenlock. The drivers were well known to us children and we always spoke to them with the utmost respect, referring to them as "Mr" when we got on and off the bus (for example, "Mr Elcock", whose company it was and who often also drove our school bus), thanking them for transporting us to and from school. In those days it was strongly impressed on us by our parents that we must at all times show respect to our elders - something which sadly seems to be lacking today.

Not far downstream from where Elcock's Coaches were located is the Lloyds Head Free Bridge, which carries the road from Ironbridge to Broseley, the latter where I lived a large part of my childhood and teenage years. The original bridge on this site was built in 1909 but by the 1980's it was struggling to cope with the ever-increasing number of vehicles on the road and, it seemed to me at the time, was always having repairs carried out on it. Therefore in the early 1990's a new bridge was commissioned and built, being opened in 1994. At the time, the design caused some controversy as it is a very modern-looking suspension design (technically known as an Asymmetric Cable Stay design) with the main span being supported by huge cables attached to a large tower on the Broseley side of the river. Many locals felt that the design was out of keeping with the heritage of the area and that a more traditional approach would have been appropriate.

About 200 yards below the Free Bridge, on the western bank, used to stand a small building made of red brick with a tile roof, which was the headquarters and practice hut of the Jackfield Brass Band. I joined the band when I was about 9 years of age and learnt to play the cornet (similar to a trumpet but shorter and making a more mellow sound), eventually becoming the assistant to the Principal Cornet. The Principal Cornet plays all the solo sections of any musical pieces and has a similar role to the leader of an orchestra. It was my job to cover for him if he couldn't be at a performance for some reason, and also to allow him breaks between solo sections of music to have a rest and regain his breath.

The band used to play at fetes, gymkhanas and carnivals all over Shropshire and we were one of the few brass bands in those days that would march as part of a carnival procession, so we were often recruited to perform this role.

The band also played at church services, particularly local Remembrance Sunday services, where it was often my task to play "The Last Post" and "Reveille" as part of the service. In fact, it was not unusual for us to be part of an outdoor service in the morning and then to play again that same evening, at a local church service.

Sadly the band hut no longer exists, the site having been sold some years ago and a private house built on it. The band re-located its headquarters to the Maws Tile Works, a mile or so downstream, which provided much more room (and some decent heating in the Winter!).

Just beyond the site of the old band hut, on the same side of the river, is a pub called The Black Swan or, as it was known to band members, the Dirty Duck. Due to the Licensing laws it was many years after I joined the band before I was allowed to enter this establishment, but at least I then realised where all the older band members disappeared to with such speed after band practice. Brass bands and pubs seem to be inextricably linked in some way, and it is said that brass band players appear to have something wrong with their legs in that they cannot pass a pub without going in!

The band hut was perched high above the river, level with the road, and whenever I was attending band practice I would gaze wistfully from the pathway to the band hut entrance at the river below, dreaming of what piscatorial adventures might be awaiting me should I be fortunate enough to be able to obtain permission to go fishing there.

Eventually I was able to obtain permission to fish, so one day in the school summer holidays I took the bus from home to Jackfield, getting off at the bus stop that was adjacent to the band hut. In those days I didn't have much tackle to carry, only my rod in its cloth rod bag, my rucksack containing reel, tackle, bait (luncheon meat), sandwiches and pop, and a small folding stool to sit on, so taking these few things on the bus was quite easy, unlike today when I think I have enough tackle to fill a bus!

As I got on the bus in Broseley the friendly driver said "going fishing are we?", which I thought was pretty obvious from what I was carrying (we hadn't done rhetorical questions at school by this time), however I smiled and nodded my head in confirmation as I gave him my bus fare and he gave me my ticket. When I got off the bus in Jackfield he wished me "good luck" and I thanked him for his kind wishes, which I hoped were a good omen for a successful day's fishing to come.

I had been looking forward to fishing this part of the river for so long that I was hugely excited to now be doing so. I walked down the band hut path and clambered down the bank to the riverside. The river was fairly low, as we had not had much rain for a few weeks, and I was able to easily find a flat area where I could pitch my little stool.

I took my two piece glass-fibre rod out of its cloth bag, together with the rod rest that was also in the bag, and tackled up. My fixed spool reel was loaded with 6lb line, which I carefully threaded through the rod rings. I had decided to fish leger-style with a drilled bullet which would roll along the bottom of the river, searching out every part of the river bed and, hopefully, passing in front of the nose of a hungry fish. My quarry was either a chub or, if I was really lucky, a barbel. A size 10 hook and a cube of luncheon meat completed the tackle, as barbel and chub love luncheon meat.

The river in front of me was flowing strongly but steadily, down to a set of rapids about 100 yards downstream. In places the surface of the river boiled, a sure sign of an underwater obstacle of some sort, either a rock or a weed bed. I cast across the river and slightly downstream, and allowed the current to roll my drilled bullet ledger downstream and slightly in towards my own bank. Once it had settled I put the rod in my rod rest, keeping the tip high to minimise the amount of line in the water and therefore keeping as tight and direct connection to my bait as possible, so that when I struck into a bite my chances of hooking the fish would be improved.

It was around late morning by now, and the sun was warm and high above me in the pale blue sky. There was hardly any breeze and I could clearly hear myriad woodland birds singing in the trees that covered the far bank – chaffinches, wood pigeons, willow warblers and thrushes. I even occasionally heard a woodpecker drumming somewhere close by, although I couldn't actually see it as it must have been well inside the thick woodland. On my own bank I was serenaded by a male blackbird perched atop the band hut above and behind me, its loud melodious warbling adding to the perfection of the day.

Bites were hard to come by so I kept re-casting to different parts of the river to try to search out as much of it as possible. Unfortunately, as a result, on a number of occasions I found myself snagged on the rocks and weed beds mentioned earlier and had to pull for a break, losing some tackle as I did so. However, this is all part and parcel of fishing so I wasn't too bothered, especially if I was able to catch something.

Lunchtime came and went, my stomach accurately informing me when lunch was due. I ate my cheese sandwiches and the apple which my mum had packed for me, washed down with a bottle of orange pop. I don't know why, but food always tastes much better when eaten in the countryside, especially when sitting alongside a river.

Just after lunch came my first bite. The rod tip jagged round and I struck into a fish. It made an initial run downstream and I allowed it to do so as I wasn't sure at that point how big it might be and I didn't want to apply too much pressure and potentially break the line. However, it soon became apparent that it was not a big fish and I was able to coax it back upstream despite it kiting in the main flow and using this to its advantage. It made a couple more dashes as I drew it towards the bank, and by this time I was pretty sure that it was a barbel. Eventually it tired and I drew it towards me. It was indeed a small barbel of about 1lb and shone golden in the sunlight as I drew it across the surface of the water and beached it in the shallows at my feet, as I had forgotten to bring my landing net with me.

It was hooked right in the corner of the mouth, so I quickly removed the hook using a disgorger and took a brief moment to admire my prize. It was a fin-perfect little barbel and I guessed that it had never been caught before as it was so pristine. It's torpedo-shaped body, orangey-red fins and underslung mouth with four barbules make the barbel unmistakeable, and I love catching them as they put up such a strong fight all the way to the net. As a result, however, they are often exhausted and need to be returned to the water quickly and carefully, so I waded into the shallows and held the fish with its nose pointing upstream, allowing oxygen from the water to run over its gills while it regained its strength. It is really important not to release them too soon as the strong flow of the river may be too much for them in their weakened state so I held it gently until it started kicking its tail strongly, whereupon I let it slip out of my hands and glide back into the depths of the river, gradually disappearing from view.

I was ecstatic at having caught a barbel and took a moment to reflect on and enjoy the experience before putting another cube of luncheon meat on the hook and re-casting to the same place as last time, which had of course resulted in a fish and which I hoped would lead to more bites as barbel tend to be a shoaling fish, especially when young. As they get older and larger they become more solitary or gather in much smaller groups.

I didn't have to wait long before the rod tip jagged round sharply again, and I struck into another fish. A similar fight to my first fish ensued and eventually I beached another small barbel of about 1lb, virtually identical in appearance to my earlier catch. Again I unhooked my prize and gently held it in the water while it regained its strength and until, with a flick of its powerful tail, it propelled itself out of my hands and back into the main part of the river.

Over the next couple of hours I caught another two barbel, making a total of four for the session, before it was time to catch the bus home. I packed my gear up and climbed up the bank back to the roadside and the bus stop, happy and content with my days fishing, catching barbel by the band hut.

Perhaps the friendly bus driver's kind wishes for my days fishing were a good omen after all.

~~~~~~~~~~

Chapter 5 – Floodwater Fishing at Atcham

~~~~~~~~~~

On a cold and grey day in late February I decided to go fishing at Atcham, a lovely stretch of the river some four miles south of the county town of Shrewsbury. The Close Season was fast approaching, and I was keen to fit in a session before fishing on the river was no longer permitted until that glorious day in June when the season starts again and anglers everywhere once again retrieve rod and reel (which have been lovingly cleaned and maintained during the close season) and race to their favourite river or lake to wet a line.

Atcham is an historical village on what used to be the main A5 London to Holyhead Road, or Watling Street to give it its Roman name as it was the Romans who upgraded what was an ancient track into a main route across the country during their occupation of Britain in AD43-AD410. Indeed, the road passes close to the former Roman city of Viriconium (or Wroxeter as it is known today), some two miles east of Atcham, which was once the fourth largest city in Roman Britain and whose impressive ruins are today managed by English Heritage.

There are two bridges across the river at Atcham. The original bridge was designed by Shropshire-born architect and civil engineer John Gwynn. Gwynn built a number of bridges over the Severn and this was his first, the others being at Llandrinio, The English Bridge in Shrewsbury, and at Worcester. The bridge was built between 1769 - 1771 to carry the Holyhead Road which in the eighteenth century was a main route for the Irish Mail coaches from London to the ferry at Holyhead on Anglesey. Gwynn designed it in a classical style to blend in with nearby Attingham Hall. The current road bridge was commissioned and constructed as the original bridge could no longer withstand the demands put on it by the increased volume of traffic using what was then the main A5 trunk road (prior to the construction of the new A5 dual carriageway further to the north, as part of the Shrewsbury bypass). The bridge was designed by L G Mouchel and construction commenced in 1927, officially opening in 1929.

I parked my car in the Mytton and Mermaid Hotel car park, which is situated on the eastern bank of the river, and walked along the footpath at the side of the A5 to purchase a day ticket from the little Atcham village shop which also doubled-up as a post office. Having obtained my ticket I walked back along the road to my car and unpacked my tackle which consisted of my 10ft ledger rod, fixed spool reel, a rucksack containing my other tackle (ledger weights, disgorger, hooks and so on) and bait box, my landing net and a small folding stool. I tried to keep tackle to a minimum as I intended to adopt a roving approach which would involve walking some way along the river, so travelling as light as possible was important.

Having collected my tackle I crossed over the river using the original eighteenth-century bridge, which is still open to pedestrians, and once on the western side I climbed over the barred gate into the field which separated the river from the minor vehicular road linking Atcham to Cross Houses.

Approaching the river I glanced upstream to the old bridge and could clearly see the remnants of last years' house martin nests under the bridge arches. If you visit here in summer the area is alive with house martins hawking up and down river and over the adjoining fields, searching for food for their young. Now, however, last years' birds were long gone to their wintering grounds in Europe but I knew that in a few months' time they would return to this place, the same place where they have nested for many years, to raise more broods.

We had had a lot of rain in recent weeks, both in Shropshire and upstream in Wales, and the river had clearly burst its banks at some time, spreading out over the adjoining fields. However, it had now receded somewhat and was contained within its banks, albeit lapping at the very top of the bank some 4 – 5 ft higher than normal.

As a result of the recent flooding the surrounding fields were still very wet and marshy, and black-headed gulls were searching in the wet soil for worms, rising as a group from the ground uttering their usual harsh "kwarr" call as something startled them, then settling back down again as a group to feed.

Overhead the sky was rather grey and darker grey clouds scudded along on a strong breeze. Down at river level the breeze was less strong, but still a little gusty at times. The temperature had risen slightly in the last few days, although was still cold enough to require warm clothing. It was this rise in temperature that had encouraged me to embark on today's session, as I was hopeful that it would cause the fish to be on the feed.

As mentioned, the river was lapping at the top of its banks and was a rather muddy brown colour due to the recent floodwater washing soil into it. It was also still pushing through at a fair rate of knots, stronger than I had anticipated, so after brief consideration of the conditions I decided I would walk downstream and try to find an area of water where the current was not so strong and where fish might be sheltering from the powerful currents.

Despite travelling lightly tackle-wise it was still hard going walking along, as the riverbank was very marshy and my wellington boots kept sinking into the mud. However, even in such conditions, I was loving being out in the countryside and at the riverside, as there is still much to observe and enjoy in Nature at this time of year as we head out of the short dark days of winter and look forward with anticipation to the new birth of spring and longer brighter days to come. Across the river I could see the ancient church of St Eata, which dates from the eleventh century. Thankfully it is built on slightly higher ground, providing some protection from the river when it is in flood.

As I continued walking downstream I came to a small semi-circular bay out of the main flow of the river, where I hoped that a few fish may have congregated out of the strong current. The river was swirling into this bay on its downstream edge, circling back to the upstream edge before it looped out into the main flow once more. I was hoping that due to this action of the water, any food being brought downstream by the river would also be washed into this little bay, and the fish would know this and be waiting there accordingly.

Taking my cue from the black headed gulls, and thinking that the fish would also have been feeding on worms when the river had burst its banks over the flooded fields, I had some lobworms with me as bait which I had dug from my garden earlier that morning. I opened my bait box and selected a large juicy worm which I hooked through the middle so that it wriggled enticingly. For a ledger weight I was using my favourite swan shot link. This consists of a simple loop of line with a number of swan shot squeezed onto the loop. The main line is threaded through the loop and then the link is stopped at the required length above the hook by a smaller shot. The beauty of this set up is that it allows me to add or take off shots until I find the correct amount of weight needed to just hold bottom. With a roving approach this is especially useful as you encounter different water conditions as you walk up and down the river, sometimes where the current is strong and sometimes where it is less strong, so the ability to speedily add or subtract weight, as required, is very convenient and means more time spent fishing rather than changing tackle from a heavier ledger to a lighter ledger, or vice versa.

Looking at the flow in the small bay, which was still quite powerful, I judged that I would need three swan shot so I quickly squeezed these into the loop of line, and a smaller shot on the main line to stop the weight about 12 inches from the hook. I decided to cast into the bay from the downstream edge as the fish would likely then be facing me into the flow so that the water could pass through their mouths and out over their gills. I reasoned that they would be unlikely to see me and be spooked because the water was such a muddy brown colour, however I stayed as low to the horizon as I could because at this point there was no tree cover behind me to help conceal my presence.

I swung out the ledger and bait and felt the current take it away from me slightly, towards the upstream edge of the bay, before coming to a stop as it settled on the riverbed. I held the line between my thumb and forefinger in order to feel for the slightest indication of a bite which, when it came, would be either a tugging on the line or perhaps even just a tremble if the bite is very cautious. Whilst either would likely be very gentle, they feel like an electric shock that suddenly has all your senses racing.

Despite my eager anticipation, after a while nothing happened so, holding the line, I lifted the rod tip slightly and felt the ledger lift off the riverbed and move slightly further away from me in the current before settling once more. Almost immediately there was a strong tug on the line and I struck into a fish. Once hooked the fish shot out of the bay and into the main river, using the strong flow to its advantage. I gave some line but the fish continued bolting downstream and because of the strong current I was powerless to stop it. I had no alternative but to follow it downstream, half walking, half running, trying to stay connected to it as it continued to use the powerful current to get away.

I must have gone at least 100 yards downstream before I felt any lessening of the fish pulling on the line. Almost imperceptibly it was slowing and I was able to regain line and draw it upstream towards me. It was only then when I suddenly realised that, in my headlong flight after the fish, I had left my landing net at the little bay.

The fish, after one or two more quick dashes downstream, was now obviously tiring and was coming in quite calmly, and I looked around me frantically to see if I had any options other than to have to walk the fish all the way back to where my landing net was, which I didn't want to do for the fish's sake as it was obviously becoming exhausted in the powerful current. I suddenly spotted a patch of riverbank just a few yards away where the water was literally lapping the top of the bank, level with the field, so I drew the fish into this spot and simply beached it by gently easing it from water to land before kneeling down to hold on to it so that I could unhook it.

In my rush I had also left my rucksack behind, which contained all my tackle including my disgorger, however I was using a barbless hook (as I always do as they cause less damage to the fishes' mouths) and the hook was clearly visible just inside the lip of the fish, so I was able to easily slip it out using my fingers.

I took a few seconds to admire my prize, which was a beautiful brassy chub of about 2lbs, before doing the reverse of what I had previously done, simply easing it from land to water at the spot where the river was lapping level with the field. I held it for a few more seconds while it gathered its breath then, with a quick flick of its tail, it was off, quickly disappearing from sight in the muddy water.

I walked back to my rucksack and landing net and re-baited with another lobworm before casting back into the little bay. However, despite searching as much of the bay as I could, I didn't get another bite so I decided to move on downstream and look for another similar fish holding spot.

I tried a number of spots along what must have been a one mile stretch of the river, but without success. The light was now starting to fade so I decided to call it a day. It was a delightful walk back upstream to the two bridges and my car, as the wind had now dropped and everything was calm and still, apart from the rushing river. In the stillness of the late afternoon I could hear a blackbird singing melodiously from somewhere across the river, perhaps from one of the tall trees by St Eata's Church, signalling the approaching end of the day. The end of the fishing season was also approaching in a couple of weeks' time, but I was already looking forward to mid-June when the new season would commence and I would once again be on the banks of the Severn, enjoying the beautiful river, the surrounding countryside, its wildlife, and its wonderful fishing.

~~~~~~~~~~

Chapter 6 – Barbel Below Buildwas Bridge

~~~~~~~~~~

Downstream of the village of Buildwas the river runs between heavily wooded banks on both sides, making it impossible to see the river from the Ironbridge Road, which sits halfway up the valley side. However, a little way into this wooded stretch the western bank suddenly opens out a little and reveals the spectacular ruins of Buildwas Abbey. The Abbey was founded 1135 as a Cistercian monastery and was built here to take advantage of the river, which at that time could be forded safely and was the major river crossing point in the area. The river also supplied water to the Abbey's monks.

Just below the Abbey the river flows under Buildwas Bridge. A bridge has existed here since medieval times and has gone through a number of iterations since. The current bridge was constructed in 1992 and carries the road from Ironbridge to Much Wenlock where, incidentally, I went to school (when I wasn't fishing).

The western bank of the river below the bridge was previously the site of the Ironbridge Power Station, opened in 1932 and de-commissioned in 2015. It has now been demolished, with the site allocated to future housing. I clearly recall as a young child being driven past the power station each Saturday night on our way to visit my Gran, who lived in nearby Madeley. I have vivid memories of the main building of the power station glowing an unearthly green colour through the large glass windows along its frontage and I remember wondering if it was in fact a huge alien space craft which had landed there.

Along the river at this point are a number of outfalls, where the water used to provide cooling in the power station cooling towers was returned to the river. I recall that these were always good places to fish in the winter months because the returned water was often a few degrees warmer than the river, so fish often congregated here, taking advantage of the extra warmth.

Just below Buildwas Bridge, on the western bank, are the power station sports fields. As a teenager I used to play football on these fields. It was a venue which all the teams in our Sunday league enjoyed playing at because the pitch was actually flat, unlike most of the pitches we played on which were usually just sloping grassy fields marked out with a pitch and goal posts, where sheep and cows grazed during the week (as a cheap way of keeping the grass down). Consequently, cow pats provided an interesting (and smelly) 'challenge' to the players, especially if you happened to fall in one.

At this point the river divides around a wooded island, with the main stream going to the western side of the island and a smaller off-shoot to the eastern side, coming back together at the end of the island some 100 yards downstream.

Where the two flows re-converged there is a favourite fishing spot of mine and my memory goes back many years to a warm summer evening spent fishing for barbel at this spot..........

After just over a decade away from Shropshire, the river, and fishing generally (due to work commitments), I returned to Shropshire in the early 1990's and felt the urge to get re-acquainted with the river and also to take up fishing again in earnest.

At the Bank office where I was working at the time, I met a young chap called Neil who, it transpired, was a keen pike fisherman. Pike fishing was something I had never tried, and we would spend our lunchtimes in the staff room talking about fishing generally, and our respective fishing preferences, his for pike and mine for barbel and chub.

We soon agreed that it would be a good idea to try each other's favoured pursuit so initially we decided upon an evening's fishing on the river for barbel. I told him that I knew of a good spot below Buildwas Bridge, where I had caught barbel before, so that was the obvious choice of venue because I really wanted him to experience hooking and landing a barbel, that most powerful of river fish.

It was a lovely summer's evening in late June when we embarked upon our trip. We had had a long dry spell, with very warm temperatures, but the weather was about to break, and thunder had been forecast for later that night.

The river was very low but the stretch we intended to fish had a fast run under the far bank which I knew would be well oxygenated and I felt sure that the fish would be attracted to this feature, thereby concentrating what fish were in that stretch into a relatively small area.

We met up at the river at 6pm, parking our cars in the small lay-by at the side of the road which runs from Buildwas to Ironbridge. From there it was simply a matter of climbing over the stile and walking across the flat field to the stretch of the river which was controlled by Telford Angling Association.

Once over the stile and shielded from the road by the thick hedge of blackthorn, all noise from any passing cars died away and all we could hear were the wood pigeons cooing in the surrounding trees and the gurgling of the river in the distance. The evening was very still and warm, and the swallows swooped low over the wide grassy field catching insects with unfailing accuracy. The sheep which were grazing in the field gave us hardly a glance as we walked quietly along. The path came to the river, and we then turned left and walked downstream to our chosen swim, the point just beyond where the flows merge after dividing around a wooded island. The island itself is about 100 yards long and 20 yards wide, covered thickly in trees and undergrowth.

As we walked along the riverside path, we looked down the steep bank into the smaller off-shoot of the main river and could see chub lazily wafting across the modest flow, intercepting whatever food came their way. They scattered in alarm as our shadows fell on the water, but we weren't too concerned as the chub weren't our intended quarry that evening. However, it was a good place to remember for another fishing expedition at a later date, particularly in the autumn and winter when the river would be well up and the fish would naturally congregate in the smaller off-shoot, away from the main flow which would be racing through full of flood water.

Just below the island on our side of the river, where the small offshoot of the river re-joined its big brother, was a long shallow run with a sandy bottom which was normally covered by water but due to the very dry conditions we had experienced lately, and the river being so low, it was now transformed into a long sandy beach which protruded out into the river. This was ideal because the river at this point is quite wide, probably 50 yards from bank to bank, and the fast run we wanted to fish was under the far bank. Usually this meant that when one cast into the faster water a large amount of line between rod tip and bait was caught by the flow of the river and the bait dragged out of position. However, the newly revealed sandy beach enabled us to be some 20 yards closer to the swim than normal, so cutting down the amount of line in the water.

We climbed down the steep bank onto the beach and set up our tackle. I had recently purchased an 11ft match rod, which was supposed to be used for float fishing on still waters, but I had discovered that the rod actually had enough power to also handle reasonably heavy ledger weights, thereby giving me a good mix of power and sensitivity. I coupled this with a fixed spool reel loaded with 8lb line in view of our intended quarry and also the power of the river which pushed through with some force at this point. I was using an Arlesey bomb as a ledger weight, just heavy enough that it would roll along the bottom of the river into the position I wanted it to settle at.

Bait was 1-inch cubes of luncheon meat fished on a number 10 Drennan Super Specialist hook, as I had found that this brand had the strength to handle strong fish such as barbel without pulling straight.

The hook was pushed right through the meat, then turned 90 degrees and the point reinserted into the bait. This would, I hoped, provide enough of a hook hold to withstand the long cast to the fast water under the far bank without the bait flying off the hook, but not too strong that it would prevent the hook taking hold when I struck into a fish. Neil was using similar tactics, copying me because he had little experience of barbel fishing.

We spaced ourselves about 10 yards apart and cast over to the far side of the river. The baits landed in the faster water, as we had intended, and the current swept them downstream and into the slightly slower water which abutted the faster water, where we thought that barbel might be holding up, waiting for the faster water to bring food to them.

I settled down on to the little fold-up stool which I carried and put the rod into a single rod rest with the tip high up so that it was easy to see against the sky above the far bank and also to try to keep as much line out of the river as possible, to prevent the current dragging it out of position.

It was a truly beautiful evening – warm and still. The sky was a little overcast, a suggestion of the thunder which had been promised for later. Wood pigeons cooed in the trees and swifts and house martins demonstrated their enviable ability for stunt flying, rising high then swooping low over the river to catch insects. We wished they had caught more midges, as these annoying little blighters had taken a fancy to Neil and me and were eating us to death, however we were both wearing caps to try to protect at least part of our heads from their bites. A flash of blue caught my eye as a kingfisher streaked upstream in front of us, flying low over the water. This part of the river teems with these beautiful birds, and I cannot remember a fishing trip when I failed to see one, such are their numbers.

We had barely got settled before the peaceful scene was rudely (but pleasurably) interrupted as my rod was literally wrenched out of the rod rest by some unseen powerful force.

Thankfully I was alert enough to grab it before it was dragged into the river, and I simply lifted into a good fish - I didn't need to strike because the fish had obviously hooked itself in the ferocity of the take.

The reel sang as the fish tore off downstream, peeling line from the spool at an alarming rate. I had 100 yards of line on the reel and started to wonder if that would be enough, when gradually the fish slowed, and I was able to recover some line back onto the spool.

However, immediately it felt me start to recover line the fish raced back upstream, with me hastily trying to take up the slack line so that my barbless hook wouldn't lose its hold. The as yet unseen torpedo powered past my position and continued upstream, no doubt heading for Shrewsbury, some 10 miles away. Again, line began to peel off the spool and there was nothing I could do to stop it – I feared that if I suddenly clamped down on the reel the line or the hook knot would surely break. It must have got some 50 yards upstream of me before it took a breather, and I was able to gently coax it back downstream towards me.

A number of times I thought I had the upper hand but each time it powered off again, upstream and downstream, with me powerless to stop it. Gradually, however, I reeled it closer and closer until it was in the shallow water in front of us and I could see that my torpedo had fins. The barbel, which I could now see clearly in the shallow water, came slowly towards me and I picked up the landing net in my left hand and slipped it into the water, intending to ease the fish over the rim of the net before lifting and claiming my prize.

However, the barbel had other ideas and despite me sliding the net into the water gently the fish obviously saw it and suddenly turned and powered off again, nearly catching me unawares. Again, line peeled off the spool and the reel sang in the quiet evening.

By this time my right arm was aching, and I began to be filled with self-doubt about whether I would actually land the fish in time to go to work the next morning. Again, we went through the process of the fish rushing downstream about 50 yards before it stopped, and I slowly recovered line. This performance was repeated a further three or four times, with ever decreasing vigour, until the fish eventually rolled on the surface in front of me and I knew that it was mine. Slipping the net under it I lifted and the barbel sagged into the mesh, completely spent from its vigorous attempts to get away.

Lowering it gently onto the soft sand I looked for the hook in its mouth, only to discover that it had fallen out in the net, as barbless hooks often do once the pressure is relaxed. I still prefer using them though, as they cause less harm to the fish's mouths.

Aware that the fish was completely spent I quickly placed it in a plastic bag brought along especially for the job (good old Sainsbury's) and weighed my beautiful prize. The scales stopped at just over 7lbs, which made it at that time the biggest barbel I had ever caught.

Slipping the fish out of the bag I waded into the shallow water and cradled it in the water with its nose pointing upstream, allowing it to fully recover before letting it swim off into the main part of the river. This is very important when barbel fishing in particular, because barbel give absolutely everything in the fight and if allowed to swim off before fully recovering are likely to not survive in the strong flow of the river.

I crouched there holding my prize and admiring the sleek shape so well suited to hugging the bottom of powerful rivers, the beautiful golden scales, wonderful crimson fins and large underslung mouth. Barbel are indeed amongst the most attractive of our native species and this one shone in the evening sunlight like a bar of gold in my hands.

Gradually, with the gentle flow of the river washing over its gills, the barbel began to recover, its tail wavering with ever increasing strength. Then, with a sudden flick of its tail, it eased out of my loose grip and sank out of sight back into the deeper water of the main part of the river.

I would have been happy if I had not caught another fish all evening but that was not to be the case. Both Neil and I continued to catch barbel at regular intervals until the light got too dark at about 9pm. Between us we must have caught at least a dozen fish, weighing between 3lbs and my fish of 7lbs, which was the best of the session. Clearly, we had been right in suspecting that the fish were bunched up on the edge of the faster water under the far bank, where the oxygen levels were at their highest.

As we walked back to our cars in the now near-darkness, tired but happy, contented with our evening, and with bats squeaking in the air around us, Neil talked about how much he had enjoyed himself and that we must go barbel fishing again, although not until after he had returned the compliment by taking me pike fishing.

As I had never been pike fishing before I quickly agreed, but unfortunately our individual commitments meant that we could not do this for a considerable time.

Tragically, Neil was killed in a motorbike accident just over a year later.

We never did go pike fishing together.

~~~~~~~~~~

Chapter 7 – A Summer Day at Monkhopton

~~~~~~~~~~

It was a very warm summer's day and I had planned to fish the river at Bridgnorth. However, we had been having a prolonged spell of dry sunny weather and the river was very low and de-oxygenated and I thought that the fishing was likely to be poor.

Therefore, I decided instead that I would visit a commercial fishing venue that I knew called Monkhall Fishery at Monkhopton.

Monkhopton is a small village located approximately 7 miles west of the River Severn at Bridgnorth. At its heart is the parish church of St Peter's surrounded by a collection of scattered farms and dwellings. It is a lovely quiet little rural village, and if you enjoy the countryside and its wildlife, it is well worth a visit.

My connection with Monkhall Fishery goes back to my time as a Bank Manager at Barclays Bank in Birmingham. The fishery was one of our customers and the Bank had assisted the then owner to create the fishery on a site that originally comprised a small farmhouse, some outbuildings, some land, and a nearby brook. Today the fishery comprises a dwelling house for the owner, the outbuildings have been converted to provide a café for anglers, and there are a total of six lakes constructed at various locations into the eastern side of the shallow valley. On a number of occasions I took some of my customers (whom I knew were keen fishermen) for an afternoon's fishing there, where we would have a friendly match amongst ourselves followed by tea in the fishery cafe.

The location of the fishery is simply wonderful. It is off the main road and therefore beautifully quiet, and because the lakes are spread out up the eastern slope of the valley they provide exquisite views south west towards the Clee Hills and Corve Dale.

I arrived at the fishery about 9.30am, having stopped off on the way at my local tackle shop to buy some maggots for bait. I also had with me some sweetcorn as an alternative. I parked up and called in at the farmhouse to pay for my day ticket and to purchase some fishery pellets. The owner advised me that the fishery was quiet today as there were no matches on, and that I could pretty much choose to fish wherever I wanted to.

Seeking tranquillity and the lovely views westwards, I chose to fish on the lake highest up the valley side, called Lark Pool, which has a nice variety of fish including carp, F1s, crucian carp, tench, roach and skimmer bream. The pool is roughly triangular-shaped, with a similar shaped island running the full length. I had the whole pool to myself so opted for a peg that had one of the corners of the island directly across from me, which are usually good fishing locations as fish often hug the island as they move around the pool. Being on a corner also meant that I had options in that I could fish directly to the island or just off the corner if that was where the fish were that day, although to do this I would have to fish a waggler as my carbon fibre pole was only 12.5m in length and wouldn't quite reach the island.

As I really wanted to fish the pole rather than the waggler, I decided to target three lines – one in the margins to my left, alternating with one in the margins to my right, and the last one 'down the track' in the deeper water approximately halfway across to the island. The latter I would either fish on the bottom or come up in the water if the fish were feeding well in the upper layers.

I set up my seat box and tackle on the purpose-built fishing platform and plumbed up the depths where I wanted to fish. In the left and right margins, tight to the reeds, I had about 18 inches of water. Down the track I had about 5 foot depth. As the two margin swims were the same depth I used the same float rig for both, on fairly strong line so that I could easily bully a hooked fish away from the reeds and out into open water. For fishing down the track I set up a lighter float rig where I could easily move the float up and down depending on what layer of water I wanted to fish in. Using Tippex I marked the plumbed depths on my pole top kits, so that I could easily set up again if the rig got broken or, in the case of the track rig, so that I could move the float up and down and still easily return to fishing on the bottom by simply moving the float back to the Tippex mark.

Even though it was now only mid-morning it was getting quite hot, as the sun blazed out of a clear blue sky. In the distance the horizon shimmered in the heat haze. Thankfully I had bought a hat with me to give my head some protection so I quickly donned this, applied some sun screen to my arms and face, and started to fish, being careful to wipe all traces of the sun screen off my hands so as not to contaminate the bait as I handled it.

I loose fed some pellets, a few maggots and a couple of grains of corn into each of my three swims, then started off on the track swim fishing on the bottom and using a single maggot as bait. Immediately it settled the float dipped under and I lifted my pole into a small roach, which came splashing to the landing net. It was a beautiful little fish, fin-perfect with silver body and red fins. I quickly slipped the barbless hook out of its lip and gently returned it to the water. I wasn't using a keep net to retain the fish in as I don't like to do so unless I am fishing a match, preferring to get them back into open water as soon as possible. Also, as it was so hot in the sunshine I thought it wouldn't be good for the fish to be in a keep net in fairly shallow water that would likely get pretty warm as the day went on.

I rebaited with another single maggot and shipped my pole out to my track swim. Again, the float had barely settled before it dipped under and another small roach came to the landing net. This process repeated until I had caught perhaps a dozen small roach. During this time, every few moments I had been loose feeding small amounts of pellets, corn and maggots in each swim so I decided to try fishing up in the water in my track swim, to see if the continual loose feeding had bought the fish off the bottom. I set the float at about half depth, some 2 – 3 feet, and re-baited with a single maggot.

I had the small split shots on my rig spread out 'shirt-button' style so that the bait fell slowly through the water, but before the float could settle it shot off to the left as something took the bait on the drop. This felt like a slightly better fish and it put up a feisty little struggle before coming to the surface where I netted it. It was a rudd of perhaps 4 ounces. I could tell it was a rudd (rather than a roach, which is quite similar) because of its upturned mouth that is perfectly designed for taking food from above the fish, either by taking it as it falls down through the water or from the surface. Indeed rudd can often be heard on warm summer evenings noisily slurping insects and the like from the surface of a lake, around lily pads and weed beds.

After returning the rudd to the water I decided it was time to give my margin swims a go. I started with the one to my left, this time using a single grain of corn as bait because I felt sure that if there were fish there they would likely be either carp or F1s, both of which love sweetcorn.

I eased the float down into the water, tight to the bankside reeds, where it settled with just the small, dumpy, orange tip showing above the water. I had been watching the reeds for any signs of movement whilst fishing my track swim, but hadn't seen anything. However this did not mean that there were no fish present, so I was still hopeful of a bite.

Suddenly, the float moved side to side slightly, without going under, and I surmised that there was a fish in my swim that had brushed against the line. I was immediately fully alert and poised ready for a bite. I didn't have to wait long before the float dived under and a bow wave indicated that a fish had taken the bait and shot out into the lake. It put up a fierce battle, repeatedly making strong dashes away from me as I tried to bring it to the waiting net. However the strong tackle was more than a match for it and eventually the fish surfaced just in front of my platform. I quickly pushed the landing net into the water underneath the fish and lifted it up, safely netting a small mirror carp of about a pound. I slipped the hook out of its mouth and took a few seconds to admire my prize. It was a very pretty little fish, in perfect condition which, I was sure, any angler would have been pleased to catch. I quickly slipped it back in the landing net then lowered the net into the water, allowing the fish to swim away.

Having disturbed the left hand margin swim by catching the carp, I decided to switch to the right hand margin to see if anything was present there. Again I baited up with a single grain of corn and lowered the bait and float into the water, tight to the reeds. I didn't have long to wait before there were signs of activity. The float dipped quickly down and back up again before starting to move away from me. I waited for a couple of seconds before lifting my pole to strike into the fish. Immediately I could feel some resistance and knew I had hooked something. This fish put up a different fight to the carp, staying low to the lake bed but still with strong dashes from time to time, so I guessed that it was a different species. It tried repeatedly to get into the reeds, but the strong tackle enabled me to keep it out of the waiting snags where I would have surely lost the fish. Eventually it came to the surface and I slipped the net under a tench of about a pound.

Tench are one of my favourite fish. They are olive green in colour with beautiful red eyes. Their scales are very small, so that the fish feels quite smooth to the touch. They are a strong fish, with a large square tail that looks a bit like a paint brush which enables them to power through the water. They are sometimes called "the doctor fish" as folklore has it that an injured fish would rub up against the tench's smooth skin so that the slime would transfer to the injured fish and cure it of its injury. Tench are evocative of warm summer mornings, at the beginning of the coarse fishing season in mid-June, fishing old estate lakes that have large water lily beds which the tench use for cover, watching the surface of the lake fizzing as the tench feed on the lake bottom and release gas that bubbles up to the surface.

Having returned the tench to the water I decided it was time to have some lunch, so I got off my box and walked up the bank behind the peg to the post and wire fence that bordered the pool and kept predators out. I sat down on the grass with my back against one of the fence posts and gazed south westwards across the green valley towards the Clee Hills. The sun was now high in the sky and I could feel its warmth on my face and skin. As I looked into the sky I could see a buzzard gracefully and effortlessly riding the air currents on motionless wings, uttering its high, plaintive mewing "pee-oo" call as it did so. I could also hear a skylark somewhere nearby with its unmistakeable sustained musical song, so wonderfully immortalised by the English composer Ralph Vaughan-Williams in his work "The Lark Ascending". I peered up into the sky and eventually spotted it, a tiny dot high in the blue yonder, and I watched it as it slowly descended singing constantly as it did so, before it dropped out of sight into the grassy field next to the fishery. The whole atmosphere was one of such beauty, warmth, peace and tranquillity that I felt as if I wanted to capture a moment of it in a bottle, as a soothing balm for the troubled times that inevitably come to us all at some point in our lives, when we simply long to be still and at peace.

The rumbling of my stomach broke into my musings and reminded me that I was supposed to be eating my lunch, which consisted of a lovely Cornish Pastie. The Cornish Pastie was reputedly adopted by Cornish tin miners in the seventeenth and eighteenth centuries as its unique shape provided a meal which could be transported easily and eaten without cutlery. Filled with meat and vegetables it also provides a complete meal in one shortcrust pastry 'shell' and I often have them for lunch when I am fishing, for these very reasons.

Returning to my fishing, I decided to once again try the track swim because by now numerous bubbles were popping on the surface of the pool, presumably as a result of something feeding on the pellets, corn and maggots that I had been loose feeding into the swim all morning.

Given that the bubbles indicated fish feeding on the bottom of the pool I reset my float so that the bait would be just touching bottom, and baited up with a single grain of corn (I avoided using maggots as these tend to be snaffled by smaller fish and I was trying to catch a better stamp of fish). I laid the float in amongst the bubbles and watched as it gradually sat upright, as the shots took the bait down, and settled with about half an inch of the black tip showing. I was using a black tip because the brightness of the sun was reflecting on the water, so a black tip was by far the easiest to see.

Nothing happened for a few moments, which I thought was unusual given the number of bubbles still popping on the surface. Then, suddenly, the float twitched slightly and the tip rose fractionally in the water, indicating that a fish had lifted the bait off the bottom and in doing so taken some weight off the float. I lifted my pole and immediately felt the resistance of a fish. It made an initial short run, pulling some of the soft elastic out of the tip of the pole then turned towards me as the tension of the elastic pulled it back towards the pole tip. I shipped back until I just had my top kit in hand and lifted the tip to bring the fish to the surface. It was a skimmer bream of about 8 ounces. I slipped the landing net under it and lifted it out of the water.

Skimmer bream or, as they are often simply called, skimmers, are essentially young bream. They are silvery in colour whereas adult bream tend to be more bronze in colour. All bream are very slimy and generally leave a coating of this on your landing net and on your line above the hook. The latter should be pulled off the line before re-casting otherwise it can affect bait presentation. Bream are a shoal fish so when you catch one you can be fairly certain that there are others in the same swim, assuming they haven't been frightened off by you catching the first one!

I slipped the fish back and rebaited with another grain of corn, shipping out to the patch of water where bubbles were still appearing on the surface, indicating that the fish were continuing to feed and hadn't been frightened off. Over the next half an hour or so I landed another six skimmers (and one roach) from the same spot, despite having missed a few really delicate bites that barely registered on the float.

By now it was fast approaching the time when I needed to head home, and it was with some reluctance (isn't it always?) that I finally stopped fishing and packed away my gear.

As I walked back to the car I reflected on what had been a great days' fishing. I had caught a mixed bag of fish including roach, rudd, tench, carp and skimmers, and all in a wonderful setting on a lovely sunny summer day. What more could any angler ask for?

~~~~~~~~~~

64

Chapter 8 – Autumn Match Fishing

~~~~~~~~~~

I hope that the reader will allow me to digress for a moment from the Severn and Shropshire to relate a story that I think has an important lesson for all anglers when they are fishing a venue for the first time, be it river or lake. The occasion was when I went match fishing at Gold Valley Lakes in Aldershot.

I don't normally do much match fishing, partly because I am not very good at it, but also because I prefer the peace and solitude I have when fishing on my own on some quiet riverbank or lakeside.

I have previously mentioned that, for various reasons, I was away from fishing for some time in my late teens and early twenties. I returned to it when working for Barclays Bank, and in the West Midlands Region of the Bank we had a fishing team that attended the annual Bank fishing competition against other regions of the Bank. This event was held at various locations around the UK and in this particular year the event was to be held in early October, at Gold Valley Lakes, a well-known venue on the match fishing circuit.

Competitors had to be at the venue by 8:30am for the draw, where each angler draws the number of their peg for that day from, on this occasion, a bucket containing all the peg numbers. The venue was some three hours' drive from my home in Shropshire, so I set out early, at about 5am, to give me a little extra margin in case I got held up in roadworks or an accident. As it happened, I had an excellent run, only starting to experience heavy traffic as I approached London and the M25, which I needed to travel on for a short time before taking the M3 west to Aldershot.

As I parked in the venue car park the weather was grey, cold and windy. Even though I was early the car park was already quite full with the competitors who had come from other regions of the Bank all over England.

Because I was early, and because I hadn't yet had anything to eat that morning, I decided to have breakfast at the excellent café at the venue. Given that I was going to skip lunch, as the match was to run from 10am to 3pm, I opted for 'the full works' – bacon, fried egg, sausage, black pudding, mushrooms, baked beans and fried bread, all washed down with a mug of steaming hot tea. After such a sumptuous feast I was ready for anything.

Draw time came, and I queued up with the other anglers to draw my peg, which found me drawn on Gold Lake. The lake is some six acres in size with depths varying between 3 – 8ft. It contains large stocks of mirror and common carp up to 30lb, plus tench, bream, crucian carp, roach, rudd and some very big perch.

After the draw I went to the onsite tackle shop to buy some bait (maggots) and also to seek advice on how to best fish the venue, as I had not been to it before. This is a good tip whenever you are fishing a venue for the first time – always seek local advice as to the best tactics and baits that are working at that time. You will find that most venue owners are more than happy to share this knowledge with you. They can usually even provide advice specific to the actual peg that you will be fishing, such is their extensive knowledge of their venue.

When I told the chap in the tackle shop which peg I had drawn, and that I only had a rod and reel to fish with as opposed to a carbon fibre pole which most match fishermen own, he advised me to fish the feeder with ground bait in the feeder and double white maggot on the hook. As it was a very windy day I was unlikely to be significantly disadvantaged using this method, compared to the pole anglers, as they were likely to have difficulty holding the pole steady in the wind, thus making good bait presentation tricky. Thanking him for his advice I purchased some white maggots (I already had some Sainsbury's breadcrumbs that I was intending to use in the feeder) and returned to my car to unload my gear.

The car park was busy with the other competitors all unloading their gear too. It resembled a fishing tackle supermarket with all the stuff they were unloading from their vehicles. No wonder they all needed wheelbarrows to carry their mountains of tackle to their peg. As I was only just getting back into fishing, and wasn't really into match fishing, I didn't have much in the way of tackle, just one modest 11ft rod that would cope with waggler fishing or casting a small feeder, fixed spool reel, landing net, keep net and seat box containing all my bits of tackle such as hooks, disgorger, spare line, floats, split shot and feeders. I unloaded my (modest) gear from the car and walked to my peg, which wasn't too far from the car park.

My peg comprised of a flat grassy bank with a concrete slab set into the grass from which to fish. I had another angler on the next peg to my right, some 10 metres away, and no one to my left. Before me the lake which, as I mentioned, was quite large was barren of features apart from an island that was much too far for me to cast to, so I decided to keep it simple and fish the feeder directly in front of me at about thirty yards out, which was about as far as I could cast with my light rod.

I poured the breadcrumbs into a shallow container and, using some water from the lake, proceeded to mix it up adding small amounts of water as I went, as I didn't want to make it too stodgy - instead I wanted to have as light and fluffy a mix as possible so that it would 'explode' on the lake bed and attract the fish into where my hook bait was sitting. Eventually I was satisfied with the mix and left it to settle while I tackled up with a small cage feeder, stopped about twelve inches from the hook by a small split shot, and a size 16 barbless hook. With a final check of my tackle, and also making sure that anything I was likely to need was easily to hand on my two side trays (for example, disgorger), I sat back to await the start of the match, trying to keep my nerves under control.

At 10am precisely the hooter went to signal the start of the match, or the 'all in' as it is known. I pushed the cage feeder down into the breadcrumb mix until it was comfortably filled, put two maggots on the hook, and cast out.

I waited for the feeder to settle before placing the rod in two rod rests, pointing straight out to where I had cast. Modern practices would have the rod set at an angle of perhaps 45^0 – 90^0, with a quiver tip to register bites as the rod tip is pulled around by the fish. However, being a bit of a traditionalist at heart, I set up a very different bite indication system comprising a large cork with a hairgrip inserted through it. The loop of the hairgrip, where it exits the cork, is attached with string to a skewer that is pushed into the ground. The other end of a hairgrip has a 'v' shaped arrangement which when one pushes the line between the arms of the 'v' grips the line, but gently enough that it is easy to pull the line out of the 'v' when striking into a fish. After casting, the line between the reel and the first rod ring is pulled downwards and clipped into the bite indicator, forming a v-shape in the line with the lowest point of the 'v' just above ground level. When a bite occurs and the fish takes line the cork rises sharply, clearly indicating the bite and a strike easily pulls the line out of the hairgrip to enable you to play the fish.

On this particular day, this type of bite indicator arrangement had the advantage of not being affected by the wind, as the indicator was placed to the right hand side of my seat box and thus shielded from the gusty wind that was blowing from left to right.

About thirty minutes into the match I had my first bite. The cork rose quickly but steadily from just above ground level and I picked up the rod out of the rod rests and struck firmly. Immediately I could tell that it was a decent fish, as it tore off across the lake and I could do nothing to stop it. Instead I steadily gave line by backwinding the reel. Most anglers use the built in clutch to allow line to be paid off the reel as a fish runs, but I prefer to de-activate the clutch and manually backwind, as I feel it gives me more control over the fish, applying more or less pressure in response to what the fish is doing.

Eventually the carp, for I was pretty sure by now that it was a carp due to the way it was fighting, slowed and I was able to turn it and start reeling it in. It made a further couple of runs when I had to give line but, overall, I was winning and it was gradually coming towards me. I couldn't be too 'gung ho' as I only had 6lb breaking strain line on my reel but, using the bend of the rod to cushion the fish's runs and lunges, it slowly but surely came near, until it was just in front of me and I was able to lift the rod tip and bring it to the surface. I slipped the net under it and lifted. The fish made a final explosive splash with its tail, but by this time it was safely in the net and was mine.

I quickly unhooked it, the barbless hook easily coming out of the fish's lip, and slipped it into my keepnet. It was a lovely common carp, which I estimated at about 5lbs in weight.

I was delighted with my start to the match, as I hadn't seen any other anglers on the lake catch anything up to that point so, re-filling the feeder and re-baiting with two maggots, I cast out again and clipped the line into the hairgrip, setting the cork indicator just above ground level.

I didn't have too long to wait before another bite, although this one was quite different to the first. The cork rose sharply a couple of inches from the ground, then stopped. I very nearly struck but instead hesitated, as I wasn't quite sure what was happening. Almost immediately the cork plummeted to the ground and I suddenly realised that the fish had initially taken the bait and moved slightly away from me, causing the cork bite indicator to rise, before turning around and moving back towards me, dislodging the feeder and causing the 'fall back' bite as the weight of the feeder was lifted off the line.

I struck and was immediately into another decent fish. Like the first fish it raced off across the lake, so I was sure that I was into another carp. I eventually turned it and began to reclaim line. It was coming in quite steadily until it was about twenty or so yards away when it suddenly bored down in a strong power dive then proceeded to sulk around in circles near the bottom of the lake. I tried to exert pressure on it but it felt heavier than my first fish so I had to be careful, especially on my relatively light tackle.

Eventually, with gradual pressure I eased it closer to me until it was just in front of my peg. I could tell where it was as it suddenly made one last lunge, causing the water to boil as it did so. After this it appeared to have had enough and came to the surface, where I eased it towards me and over the sunken landing net. Once it was safely over the rim I lifted the net and the fish was mine.

It was another common carp which was, as I had suspected, slightly larger than the first carp. I estimated it at about 8lbs. Again, the barbless hook came out easily and I slipped the fish into the keepnet.

The wind had increased in strength by now and was making fishing tricky, especially for anglers fishing the pole, as the chap to my right was doing. He was really struggling to hold the pole steady in the wind, so after a while I noticed that he had swapped on to the waggler.

I made the mistake of thinking he must be a good angler as he had all the right gear, so about two hours into the five hour match I also switched to the waggler. However, after a bite-less hour (for both of us) I realised that I had been

71

foolish to change away from a method that was bringing me a measure of success, so I quickly went back on the feeder.

Almost immediately I was rewarded with another decent carp of about 6lbs, this time a beautiful partially scaled mirror carp, which joined its compatriots in my keep net.

As is often the case with matches (and with fishing generally) the time seemed to fly by and, before I knew it, the hooter sounded again for 'all out' and the match was over.

I packed my gear away and sat on my box waiting for the scales men to come around to weigh my catch. As anyone who has been match fishing knows, the objective is to have the biggest total weight of fish in order to win the match. There are also usually prizes for the highest weight in each section of anglers. This allows someone to win a prize even if they are in a relatively poorly performing area of a lake or river, as they only need to be the best angler in that section. In this match we had ten sections of ten anglers per section.

I had no idea how I had done overall, but I knew that I had six decent carp so was guessing that I had about 30lbs in total. I was pretty sure that the chap to my right hadn't caught that much, as I had only seen him land a couple of small carp. However, as there were approximately 100 anglers in the match, on different lakes, it was impossible to know how I stood in terms of the overall outcome.

The scales men arrived at my peg and I lifted my keep net out of the water, carrying it to where the scales were set up. As I did so, I could hear appreciative murmurings from the scales men. I tipped my fish into the weighing net and the scales men lifted it onto the scales. The needle swung around the dial and settled on 35lbs. I would later find out that this meant fifth place in the match. The chap to my right who had all the right fishing gear was not impressed, as he weighed in a mere 4lbs!

At the awards dinner that evening I received a trophy, my first ever fishing trophy, and prize money of approximately £60 which, in those days, was a decent amount of money and certainly enough to more than pay for the petrol to travel to and from the match. As we say in Shropshire, I was 'chuffed to bits'!

Later that evening, as I reflected on the day, I remembered the advice that the chap in the onsite tackle shop had told me before the match. It just goes to show the value of seeking local knowledge and advice on a venue that you have not fished before, as I am sure that this was key to my success.

~~~~~~~~~~

Chapter 9 – Midwinter Madness Near Bewdley

~~~~~~~~~~

At the town of Bewdley, just below the river bridge which was built in 1798 and designed by the renowned civil engineer Thomas Telford (1757 – 1834), is a place which I understand it was possible, many years ago, to wade across the river. My wife's family, who come from near here, clearly remember that it was possible to ford the river at this point from the grassy lawns on the eastern bank to the old wharf and Georgian-style houses on the western bank.

These days, of course, it is no longer possible to wade across the river at this point, as the river has grown deeper over the years, perhaps as a result of the heavy flood waters which regularly pass through Bewdley. Until the building of flood defences in the first decade of the twenty-first century it had become a common occurrence for the riverside houses to be flooded each year.

One July day, my wife and I were leaning on the railings on the old wharf, looking down into the river and watching small chub in the shallows as they moved upstream, paused, then turned and swam with the flow downstream maybe 10 yards or so, before turning and coming back upstream to their favourite station. They did this time and time again, unerringly coming back to the same location directly in front of us, occasionally being spooked by the seagulls that flew low over the water and which sometimes landed on the surface to pick up the occasional piece of bread thrown in by people sat on the bench seats having their lunch. People were in short sleeves and cool tops, as the day was beautifully sunny and warm - quite the opposite of a day's fishing I had near here not too long ago..............

My wife and I were staying with my parents-in-law at Kidderminster (some 3 miles from Bewdley) for a few days in early January one year. For various reasons I wasn't going to be able to go fishing again for some time in the future so only had one day when I could try out the new fishing pole I had recently acquired. It was carbon fibre in construction and 11 metres long, and I was desperate to give it a wetting.

Britain was at that time experiencing a prolonged spell of very cold weather. Over the past week the maximum temperature had struggled to reach 2 degrees Celsius, and the nights were consistently well below freezing. Also, mid-Wales, where the Severn has its source, had been experiencing snow and heavy rain, which had swept downstream to swell the river to flood proportions, overflowing the eastern bank at Bewdley and close to breaching the wharf on the western bank.

In conditions such as these I knew that a commercial fishery was my best chance of sport, and it would at least provide the opportunity to try out my new pole. I telephoned a few fisheries in the area and eventually settled on one near Worcester, some 10 miles from my parents-in-law's house.

I didn't rush to be up early to go fishing, as I would normally do in the summer, because often in winter the fish only come on to feed during the middle of the day, when the temperature is highest and the sun at its peak. Therefore, I set out around 10am and called in at the tackle shop in Kidderminster to purchase my bait, which was to be maggots, before pointing the car's nose south towards the fishery.

As I drove along, the car's onboard computer was telling me that the outside temperature was minus five degrees Celsius, and the ice warning light blinked at me persistently. Despite this I was in high spirits as I travelled through a winter wonderland of fields and hedgerows fixed in a thick coating of frost, as though God had dusted the whole world with icing sugar. The sky was clear and blue, there was little wind, and the sun was bravely attempting to make inroads into the frozen landscape, without much success.

Arriving at the fishery I parked in the car park and paid for my day ticket at the fishery shop. The fishery owner clearly thought I was barmy going fishing on such a cold day, but was obviously happy to take my money anyway. He informed me that the pool I was to fish was along a little lane beyond the shop, and that I could drive to my peg.

Fisheries which enable patrons to drive all the way to their peg are to be congratulated, as it makes fishing so much more accessible to anglers with disabilities, who are unable to walk long distances from a car park to their peg staggering, as we all do, under the weight of our tackle boxes, rod holdalls, net bags and all the other paraphernalia of the modern fisherman.

The lane beyond the shop was narrow and consisted of two well-worn wheel ruts with a grassy strip in between, with a wonderfully tangled hedgerow of hawthorn on one side and a grassy bank up to the fishing pools on the other. Normally the wheel ruts would be a holding place for water, and indeed there was water present, albeit so frozen that even the weight of the car failed to break through the ice. With the hedgerow on one side and the high bank on the other, the lane received very little sunlight at that time of year, with the sun so low in the sky, so the water remained frozen all day.

After travelling a short way along the lane, I turned right up a track through the high bank and on reaching the top could see the pool immediately in front and to the left of me. My peg was on the near-side bank of the pool, about three-quarters of the way along its length. The pool was fitted with an aerator device, which in summer provides much needed oxygen in the water for the fish. What it was now doing was providing a slight ripple on the surface of the pool which meant that the majority of it was ice free, except for the first yard or so around the edge.

I parked the car, excitedly hopped out and started unpacking my gear from the boot.

No matter how many years I have been fishing, the arrival on the bank side still evokes a great sense of excitement and anticipation in me. What will the fishing be like today? Will I catch my target species? How will I fish my swim? All these thoughts were whirling through my mind as I hurriedly unloaded the boot of the car, so much so that I clean forgot to keep myself warm.

In the nice warm car I had worn jeans and a fleecy sweater and been very cosy. Now outside in minus five degrees of cold, I was fast turning blue. I quickly located my winter weather clothing, which consisted of two pairs of socks worn inside my wellington boots, a pair of windproof over-trousers worn over my jeans, a fleecy jacket, and lastly my father-in-law's old shooting jacket which was windproof and also had a wonderfully warm furry lining. This whole ensemble was topped off by a woollen hat pulled down over my ears and a pair of neoprene gloves which have the fingertips cut off so that I can still tie knots, bait hooks and generally fish without having to take the gloves off all the time.

Now protected from the cold, I completed unloading the car and set myself up on my peg, which consisted of a gravel platform about one yard wide, in a gap between low bushes. Excitedly I took my pole sections out of their case and fitted them together until I had the full 11 metres at my disposal, resting between a pole roller behind me and the side tray of my tackle box, by my right hand.

I had prepared my rig the night before and had it tied on a pole winder ready to be fixed to the connector which was attached to the pole elastic. The float had a very fine tip as I knew bites today would be very delicate and would not register very well on a float with a thicker tip. Quickly plumbing the depth, I discovered that the bank shelved quite steadily to a depth of about four feet, at approximately six feet out from the side of the pool, before levelling off at that depth for as far as I could plumb with my pole.

I set the float at about 2 inches over depth so as to fix the bait hard to the bottom of the pool. Given the cold weather and water temperature, I felt it was unlikely that the fish would be feeding up in the water today and that my best chance came with anchoring my bait on the bottom of the pool, to give the fish plenty of time to inspect it before sucking it into their mouths.

I bulked the tiny split shot approximately two-thirds of the way down the line, with three tiny dropper shots between there and the hook, the last shot being some 10 inches from the hook itself. By bulking the majority of the shot well down the line, the bait would be quickly taken to the bottom and not waste time falling slowly through layers of water where I was sure there would be no fish because of the cold water temperature.

Baiting the tiny size 20 hook with a single maggot I shipped out the pole until I was fishing at my chosen distance, approximately 10 metres out from the bank, in the path of the rippling water flowing from the aerator. Every few minutes I fired a small number of loose maggots with a catapult into the swim, using the float as a marker. "Little and often" is a sound policy when loose feeding bait into a swim although in winter it is appropriate to feed slightly less often and with a smaller amount of bait than one would in summer, when the fish are generally feeding more actively.

The fine orange tip of the float looked splendid bobbing slightly in the rippling water and I smiled to myself and inwardly thanked God for such a beautiful day. The sun was warm on my back and with no wind to add chill to the already cold day, I was thoroughly enjoying myself.

After a short while with no bites, I was conscious that the float was being towed slightly towards the aerator, which was on my right. While the surface water appeared to be moving right to left, pushed along by the flow from the aerator, this was obviously causing an undertow moving in the opposite direction.

As already mentioned, I knew that on a day such as today I needed to anchor the bait solidly to the bottom of the pool, so I shipped the pole back in and increased the length between the float and the hook to approximately 3 inches over depth.

Shipping back out and allowing the float to settle I was still experiencing some movement of the float so I repeated the process until I had approximately 5 inches of line on the bottom of the pool, at which point the float was no longer being towed by the current and remained perfectly still. I now knew that the bait was holding in one spot, giving any interested fish plenty of time to make up its mind to decide that a juicy maggot was its ideal lunch, for by now it was midday.

I continued to loose-feed maggots into the swim, a few at a time, and just as I had fired some in and put the catapult down in my right-hand side tray, which also contained the maggots, I was conscious of a minute movement of the float, so minute that it was almost imperceptible. Anglers talk of that electric moment when the float first moves, and this was no exception. Instantly I was completely focused and alert, heart quickening slightly, and staring hard at the little orange tip sticking up out of the water.

Sure enough, there it was again, a very slight dipping of the tip. Heart beating even faster, I resisted the temptation to strike, wanting to be sure of the bite. This time the float tip slowly dipped further until only the merest fraction was showing above the water. I gently, but firmly, raised the pole and immediately felt something on the end of the line.

It was not a huge fish but enough to slightly stretch the very light elastic I had in the top section of the pole. However, I didn't mind; it was a fish and that was the main thing.

I shipped the pole back, taking the sections apart until I just had the top three sections in my right hand, a length of about 3-4 yards in total. Gentle pressure lifted the fish to the surface, where it turned on its side and came easily into the bank.

I picked up my landing net in my left hand and reached out beyond the frozen water at the edge of the pool. Even when the fish is small, I don't like lifting them out, and prefer to use a landing net for a number of reasons – the risk of losing the fish if the light tackle should give way, or possible damage to the fish's mouth by having its weight hanging on the hook. Indeed, in many commercial fisheries it is a rule that a landing net must be used when landing any fish, irrespective of its size.

Having successfully manoeuvred the fish over the rim of the landing net I lifted and bought my prize in. It was a ruffe (sometimes also called a pope), about 4 inches long and quite portly, olive brown in colour with blueish mottled spots along its sides, and a large spiny dorsal fin, somewhat reminiscent of a perch. They can grow up to nearly 10 inches in length, but at about 4 inches mine was average for the species.

I know that some anglers are dismissive of ruffe but I think they are a pretty little fish. They are also an aggressive little fish and remind me of some of the short midfielders from 70's and 80's football teams, such as Billy Bremner, who may have been small but were hard as nails.

I quickly removed the barbless hook, which came out easily, and popped the fish back in the landing net. Reaching beyond the frozen water's edge, I gently submerged the net, and the fish swam away back into the depths.

Feeling well pleased with myself, I re-baited and set about catching more fish, which I hoped were now coming on to the feed as the day reached its zenith of light and warmth (although probably still no more than zero degrees Celsius!).

Over the next two hours I caught a further four fish – two perch and two roach – the best of which was a roach of just under half a pound, a beautiful fish in pristine condition with its blueish-silvery flanks and red fins sparkling in the sunlight.

Whilst none of my catch was huge, I was still delighted with the outcome, as I knew catching anything in the challenging conditions was going to be difficult. Even the fishery owner raised his eyebrows when I told him what I had caught, as he came along for a little chat towards the end of the afternoon - perhaps he thought I was spinning him a typical fisherman's exaggerated tale. I think he also still thought of me as barmy, as he had done so when I first arrived and paid him for my day ticket.

A further delight during this wonderful fishing session was a visit from a tiny wren. While sitting still, watching my float, I became aware of a movement in the low bushes to my right. Not moving my head, I glanced slowly sideways and saw a tiny brown wren hopping from branch to branch, about a yard away.

He was no more than a couple of inches long (they are one of Britain's smallest birds) with a remarkably fine, slightly down-turned, needle-like beak. His short tail was jauntily cocked up (a readily distinguishable feature of the species) and he was gradually moving closer towards me through the bushes, as though unsure whether to approach or not.

Suddenly he flitted out of the bushes and onto the frosty ground behind my right shoulder. Moving very slowly I swivelled slightly so that I could still see him. Next thing I knew he hopped up onto the edge of my side tray full of maggots, inches away from me, and proceeded to look alternately up at me and down at the juicy maggots, as though wondering if he could get away with stealing a few, his bright black eye twinkling mischievously as he did so.

Finally making up his mind, he hopped down into the tray and grabbed a maggot in his fine bill, before flying off to the bushes to enjoy his meal.

A few moments later he was back and the whole scene was enacted again, the gradual moving closer through the bushes, the hop down onto the ground behind me, up onto the edge of the side tray, into the tray for a maggot and away to the bushes.

No proper angler begrudges a bird some of his maggots on a cold winter's day, and I smiled at the little comedy being played out with my tiny friend. In all, he came back half a dozen times before obviously having his fill and flying off into the bushes, presumably to have an afternoon nap.

As I packed up at the end of my session, I sprinkled a few maggots on the ground around my peg, and immediately a robin and a blackbird appeared and set about squabbling over this prize. By now the temperature was plunging rapidly and I was happy to provide the birds with some additional sustenance to help them through this prolonged cold spell, which can have a devastating effect on populations of smaller birds such as robins and wrens.

Quickly packing my gear away, I climbed back into the car, turned the heater on full and set off back to my parents-in-law's home. The sun was starting to set, and the western sky was turning a fiery red. It was clearly going to be another bitterly cold night but as the warmth of the car heater soaked into my body, I couldn't be happier. I had enjoyed a day's fishing in glorious winter weather, wetted my new fishing pole, caught some fish, and been delighted by the sights and sounds of the winter countryside – even if the fishery owner still thought I was barmy.

~~~~~~~~~~

Chapter 10 – Chub and Barbel at Ribbesford

~~~~~~~~~~

In the current season of my life I am living overseas, in Australia. This means that, at the moment, I am only able to visit the river during annual trips home to see family and friends (and to do some fishing!). To take advantage of the best weather (and so that I can fit as much fishing in as possible) these annual trips are usually undertaken in July or August. During one visit I was able to fit in an early morning session on the river at Bewdley.

I was going to fish at Ribbesford, just downstream of Bewdley, at a place where the bridge carrying the Bewdley Bypass crosses the river. The bridge was opened in 1987 and one of the support piers stands on a natural island on the western side of the river, where the river splits in two and a small offshoot runs between the island and the riverbank. I knew from past experience that this small offshoot of the main river held chub and, occasionally, barbel which like the steady glides over a gravelly riverbed. Also, because the island and the high riverbank are very overgrown few people take the trouble to get down to the level of the river, so the fish are largely undisturbed, and the trees and bushes reach out over the water providing shelter and a source of food such as insects falling into the water.

It was about 6am on a lovely still, sunny morning when I parked in the Blackstone Riverside Car Park, on the western side of the river. From there it was a walk of some 300 metres down through the deciduous wood to the riverbank.

I was the only person around and the wood was alive with early morning birdsong, including blackbirds, chaffinches, great tits, wrens, wood pigeons and rooks. I also saw rabbits playing on the steep bank alongside the pathway where, judging by the number of holes in the bank, they had their warren.

I emerged from the woodland just underneath the road bridge carrying the Bewdley Bypass, which towered above me. The river was quite loud at this point as it ran swiftly over the narrow shallows between the island and the riverbank, the sound echoing around off the two concrete piers (one on the island opposite me and one on the riverbank behind me) and the bridge above.

My plan this morning was to adopt a roving approach from the bridge to perhaps 250 metres downstream. The river has numbered fishing pegs along this stretch, created by the local angling club which has the fishing rights, so I decided to try each peg as I went along. Once I got to the bottom of the stretch I would turn around and fish each peg again on my way back upstream to the bridge. The river was at its normal summer height which meant that each peg had to be reached by turning off the riverbank footpath and making your way through trees, bushes and nettles to reach the water.

Because I was going to be roving I was travelling light tackle-wise. I had a small nine foot ledgering rod and fixed spool reel loaded with 6lb line. The small rod was purposely chosen because of the amount of overhanging trees and bushes which would make handling and casting a larger rod problematical. The fairly strong 6lb line was also carefully chosen because the bushes pushed their roots and branches out into the river from the bankside, creating numerous convenient snags for the fish to head for when hooked. The strong line would hopefully enable me to stop them getting into those.

End tackle was also going to be very simple, comprising my favourite swan shot link ledger stopped above the hook by another split shot, and a size 12 hook tied directly to the reel line. Bait was to be luncheon meat, which I had cut up into approximately 1cm cubes the evening before. These would be just about the right size to fully bury the hook into so that the fish would not see the hook and ignore the bait.

I started off directly underneath the bridge. At this point the side stream turns diagonally right off the main river and runs strongly over some shallows before turning sharply left as it hits the concrete retaining wall of the riverbank. A few days earlier I had walked the stretch and spotted a decent chub lying just where the side stream turns after hitting the retaining wall, so the plan was to trundle a cube of luncheon meat downstream, over the shallows, to the chub's lair.

Izaak Walton (1593 – 1683), best known for his book "The Compleat Angler", referred to the chub as "the fearfullest of fishes", as the slightest sight of a fisherman against the skyline, or human shadow on the water, or heavy footfall on the riverbank, is enough to make them drift away to a safer place. Therefore, I quietly crept into position at the head of the side stream and cast slightly downstream towards where I had seen the chub on my earlier reconnoitre. The three swan shots on my link ledger quickly took the luncheon meat cube down to the riverbed and also provided enough weight to just hold bottom.

After a couple of minutes without a bite I lifted the rod tip slightly and felt the link ledger lift off the riverbed. I paid out some line off the reel to allow the ledger and bait to trundle a little further down the swim and settle on the bottom again.

Again, after a few minutes with no bites, I repeated the process of lifting the rod tip to dislodge the weight and bait, trundling it a little further downstream again. This time there was no need to wait as the cube of luncheon meat was intercepted by a fish.

Initially I could feel slight tugs on the line, which I was holding between my thumb and forefinger, but these quickly developed into a good solid tug so I struck. The rod tip hooped over as the fish tried to use the strong flow to its advantage by heading off downstream. I initially gave it some line but quickly felt it wasn't a massive fish and, therefore, that I could afford to bully it quite strongly given the 6lb line on my reel.

The fish jagged and pulled, but to no avail, and it soon appeared out of the churning water of the shallows on to the surface and I was able to slip the landing net under it.

It was a lovely brassy chub of about 2lbs. I quickly slipped out the barbless hook and held it in the water's edge while it recovered. It wasn't long before, with a sharp flick of its tail, it shot off back into the shallows and back to its lair. Perhaps for a little while it would think twice about eating luncheon meat again.

As this swim was now thoroughly disturbed I climbed back up the bank and moved downstream to the next swim, which was just on the other side of the bridge where the side stream slowed a little and narrowed as it flowed between the overgrown island and the river bank.

This swim was really difficult to fish, for a number of reasons. The bankside vegetation was thick with shoulder-high nettles, great willowherb and cow parsley, and whilst the path initially sloped downwards fairly gently through the undergrowth the last metre or so presented a cliff-like drop to the river. There was a minute beach of gravelly soil at the bottom of this little cliff but there was no way I could get down there quietly and without scaring any fish, so I decided I would fish from half way up the bank, some two metres above the river. If I hooked something I would then worry about how I was going to land it.

I crept into position, keeping my head low and in line with the top of the undergrowth so as not to spook any fish. I then slowly raised my head so that I could see down into the river, which was about 10 metres wide at this point. Being at such a high position above the river gave me a clear view down into the water through the surface glare, and I was rewarded with a pair of fantastic visions.

To my left there was a depression in the riverbed where the winter floods had plunged down from the fast shallows upstream and carved out the bottom, before gradually rising up and across some gravelly shallows. In this hole sat two big chub, patiently waiting for food morsels to float downstream to them, their fins slowly wafting in the flow to enable them to hold position. I estimated them at maybe 4lbs each.

To my right, where the water flowed over the gravelly shallows I could see a shoal of smaller chub, maybe ten in number, holding station in the steady flow and intercepting any morsels that got past their bigger cousins upstream. Occasionally they would turn downstream and go with the flow out of my sight, but it was not very long before they appeared again, swimming upstream and returning to their station.

My initial thought was to try for one of the bigger fish in the depression in the riverbed, but I quickly had to dispel this. There was an iron structure of some sort, perhaps the remains of an old fishing platform which had been washed away by the winter floods, that stuck out across the river directly above where the chub were sitting. From my position I would have needed to cast upstream, probably underarm, and try to squeeze the bait between the surface of the river and the iron structure above without getting caught up on the iron bars, which would have inevitably led to me having to pull for a break, losing my tackle, and spooking the chub. So, somewhat reluctantly, I opted to try for one of the smaller chub to my right.

While I was keeping low amongst the undergrowth and looking down at my hands as I quietly put a cube of luncheon meat on the hook, I was suddenly aware of a quick movement of something to my left. I slowly looked up and, to my amazement, two kingfishers were sat on the iron structure that stuck out across the river, looking down into the river where the two big chub were stationed. They were perhaps 2m – 3m from where I was crouched and obviously hadn't seen me. I, however, could see every detail of their bright iridescent blue and emerald back and chestnut breast, and was simply mesmerised by their beauty. They sat there for a few moments, bobbing up and down on their iron perch, looking down into the water, before obviously deciding that the chub were too big even for them, and suddenly darting off upstream to look for more manageably-sized food.

Smiling quietly to myself at my good fortune of seeing such beautiful birds at such close quarters, I returned to my fishing. My plan was to execute a gentle underarm swing to plop the cube of luncheon meat into the water slightly to my right, from where I would gradually trundle it downstream across the gravel to the waiting shoal, imitating as best as I could a bait naturally skipping along the bottom of the river in the flow.

I had trees, bushes and nettles all around me and was also trying to make as little movement as possible so as not to scare the fish, so an underarm swing of the bait into the river was not as easy as it sounds. After a couple of deep breaths, I managed to get the bait swinging nicely, pendulum-like, and after a couple of swings to and fro I lifted my forefinger which was trapping the line and the bait swung gently outwards and plopped into the river, exactly where I had intended.

However, this is where my carefully laid plan came to a sudden end. Immediately the bait hit the water it was grabbed by something. Perhaps one of the larger chub from the upstream depression had heard the bait hit the water, turned and snaffled it, but whatever had grabbed the bait I was in big trouble as it powered away like a steam train for the snags on the island side of the stream, some 10 metres away, where trees and bushes came down right into the water.

Given the tight confines I was fishing in and the very short distance between where the fish was hooked and the snags on the island, I had no choice but to clamp down on the reel to try to stop the fish's run. The rod hooped over sharply before the line parted and I was left holding the rod and now slack line, gasping at how quickly it had all happened.

All the commotion had spooked every fish in the swim and, as I peered down into the water again there was not a fin to be seen anywhere so I decided to move on to the next swim downstream, but not before I threw in a few cubes of luncheon meat as freewill offerings, as I intended to return to this swim as I moved my way back upstream later in the session.

As I walked to the next peg downstream I looked across the river to the high red sandstone bluff that towers over the water at this point to see if I could spot the peregrine falcons that nested on the cliff face. I had heard them earlier, with their distinctive "we-chew" call but, on this occasion, I did not see them. If I had been birdwatching instead of fishing I would have sat down and patiently waited for a sighting of them, but today my main focus was fishing so I moved on downstream.

Over the next couple of hours I fished some ten separate pegs and swims downstream but apart from some fry nibbling at my luncheon meat cubes I had no success, so I started to make my way back upstream to where I had started from, under the bridge.

I didn't bother with the swims that had been no good on my way downstream, as I felt sure that they would not have improved in the meantime. Instead I headed for the swim where the chub (at least I think that is what it was) had broken me earlier and where I had scattered some free offerings of luncheon meat.

I crept through the nettles, great willowherb and cow parsley once more, and raised my head slightly so that I could see down into the water. The two larger chub had gone, but I was delighted to see that the shoal of smaller chub had returned to the gravelly shallows to my right.

Baiting up with another cube of luncheon meat I cast underarm just in front of me. The current took the bait towards the chub, and I gently coaxed it along the riverbed until it was nearly in front of their noses. Unfortunately, just as it got there something spooked them and they turned, as one, downstream and out of sight.

I was left wondering what to do. Should I sit it out and hope they would return soon, or should I call it a day (as this was the last swim I was going to fish)? However, as I was trying to make up my mind, I beheld a wonderful sight. A huge submarine-shaped fish appeared, swimming upstream, its triangular red fins helping it to easily hug the riverbed in the current while it searched for food. It was a big barbel. I held my breath as it slowly got closer and closer to my cube of luncheon meat, and had a clear view as it swam directly over the bait and snaffled it.

I struck and it immediately turned and tore off downstream at a rate of knots. It was pulling so strongly that I had to give it line, otherwise I would have risked a break. It must have gone some 50 metres downstream before it slowed slightly and I was able to turn it and gradually haul it back upstream towards me.

It used every bit of the current to try to resist me, and three times managed to turn and tear off downstream again. Each time I was forced to give line until it slowed slightly and I was once again able to turn it and bring it back upstream.

After maybe 15 – 20 minutes' battle the barbel was spent, coming up to the surface and rolling on its side. I now had to figure out how I was going to land it! As I mentioned earlier, the riverbank at this point sloped gradually downwards but the last metre or so was a sheer drop to a small gravelly beach. Picking up my landing net in my left hand, with rod still in right hand, I sat down at the top of the little cliff, with my legs hanging over, and slid down to the beach on my bottom, just managing to avoid overshooting into the river.

Amazingly, despite this somewhat undignified performance, I was still connected to the barbel so I eased it towards me and the submerged head of my landing net. Once the barbel was over the net I tried to raise it, only to realise that the fish was longer than the diameter of the net head. Unfortunately I had not anticipated catching such a large fish that morning, so had only bought with me my smaller-headed landing net, which would have been perfectly adequate for any chub or small barbel that I might have caught, but not for this monster. Trying not to panic I again eased the fish over the net and somehow managed to get it to fold its body so that it fitted in the mesh.

Hauling the net back to the riverbank I lifted it out by the net head, because I am sure that I would have broken the carbon fibre landing net handle if I had tried to lift it out that way, and placed it down on a silty bit of river bed, just in the shallows, to avoid putting it on the gravelly beach that I was stood on.

Falling on my prize I quickly removed the barbless hook with my fingers. The fish lay there, exhausted, so I was able to take a few seconds to admire it. It was beautiful, and shone like gold in the late morning sunlight. I quickly weighed it in the net – the scales stopped at just over 7lbs, one of my biggest ever barbel – before wading into the water slightly so that I could hold it in the flow, facing upstream, until it gathered its strength. This is so important when barbel fishing as they give everything in the fight and if returned to the fast water in their exhausted state would risk them not surviving.

It lay in the water with my hands underneath it, supporting it and gently holding it, as the current flowed through its mouth and over its gills, for a good 60 – 90 seconds until I could feel that it was getting ready to go. With a gentle but determined sweep of its tail it eased out of my hands and back into the main flow, immediately turning downstream and quickly disappearing from view.

I clambered back up the bank to the riverside footpath and paused for a moment, re-living the memories of that lovely morning's fishing, the wonderful fish that I had been blessed to catch, and the beautiful nature that I had seen and heard, such as the kingfishers and the peregrine falcon, before walking back through the wood to the car park and my car, and heading home. It truly had been a memorable morning.

I was due to fly home to Australia a day or two later, but I was already looking forward to returning to the river on my next visit to England to enjoy its wildlife and its fishing once again.

~~~~~~~~~~~

Chapter 11 – Match Fishing on the Flash

~~~~~~~~~~

Priorslee Flash, or "The Flash" as it is known locally, is located on the eastern outskirts of Telford, sandwiched between the main A5 trunk road (the old Roman road called Watling Street) and the M54 motorway, which both run through the middle of the town.

Telford is a 'new town' created in the 1960s - 1970s through the amalgamation and expansion of old towns and villages such as Wellington, Oakengates, Dawley and Madeley (where I was born). I believe it is now one of the fastest growing towns in Britain. The area was heavily industrialised until the second half of the twentieth century, including activities such as coal mining, iron smelting and brick making, although all of these industries have since closed down.

The town was named after the famous civil engineer Thomas Telford (1757 – 1834) who was for a time the County Surveyor for Shropshire, during which he was responsible for many road and canal projects. He is also known for other major infrastructure projects including the amazing Pontcysyllte Aqueduct near the Welsh town of Llangollen, and the Caledonian Canal in his native Scotland. He is buried in the nave of Westminster Abbey, befitting his hugely important contribution to civil engineering in Britain.

The Flash was originally two pools separated by a causeway that carried the old mineral railway line from the Lilleshall Furnaces at Priorslee. One of the pools was rather macabrely known as Hangman's Pool (I am not sure why it gained this name!). When the area was redeveloped in the 1960s - 1970s the causeway was substantially reduced in height, allowing the two pools to become one.

For a number of years my wife and I lived at Priorslee and used to regularly walk around The Flash. I also used to fish it quite often, given that it was less than 5 minutes' drive from home. It has a good mixed stock of fish including carp, roach, bream, tench, perch and pike, so provided a good variety depending on which species you were targeting at any given time of year.

The lake is also a birdwatcher's paradise including species such as heron, mallard, canada geese, mute swan, coot, moorhen, cormorant, tufted duck, great crested grebe and mandarin duck. The woodlands to the south-east and north-west of the lake are also very prolific, with species such as chaffinch, greenfinch, rook, magpie, jay, wren, greater spotted woodpecker, green woodpecker, tree creeper, willow warbler, great tit, blue tit and nuthatch all regularly to be heard or observed.

One early September day I was intending to fish for barbel and chub on the Severn, but when walking around The Flash a few days earlier I had bumped into the water bailiff, who everyone knew as Twizzle (I never did find out his real name!), and he told me that there was to be a small open match on the Flash that coming Saturday, so I changed my mind and decided to fish the match instead. I guessed that a number of the anglers who regularly fished the pool for pleasure, and whom I had got to know over the years, would be taking part so it would also be an opportunity to catch up with them and have a bit of fun competing against them in the match.

The day of the match was a lovely autumn day. The poet Keats perfectly encapsulated the sense of Autumn when he described it as a "season of mists and mellow fruitfulness". This morning was no exception. There had been an early mist, which was now beginning to dissipate in the weak sunshine, and a heavy dew which had coated the grass and hedgerows and made the spiders' webs sparkle in the sunshine like delicate silver chains. The hedgerows were also full of ripening blackberries, where birds competed with the local children to see who could eat them first.

Despite the early mist the air held a promise of a warm still day to come. Consequently, by mid-morning the sky was blue with occasional fluffy white clouds, and hardly any wind. Excellent fishing conditions for our match!

The five-hour match started at 9am but competitors had to be there by 8am for the draw to find out which peg we would be fishing on. I drew a peg on a slight promontory, with open water in front of me, a large island (the only one on the lake) diagonally to my right and the old (now submerged) causeway somewhere slightly to my left, giving me plenty of options as to where to fish.

For bait I had bought maggots and sweetcorn. Maggots are a reliable all-round bait as almost every fish that swims loves them, and I figured that I would start on these to try to put some initial fish in my net before contemplating switching to corn to try to target a better stamp of fish, such as tench, bream or larger roach.

I set up my seat box and pole. I had decided to start on the pole, directly in front of me in the open water at about 6 metres, targeting roach and, hopefully, tench which I knew patrolled along this bank in early morning. I had about 5ft of water at this spot so the pole provided me with the best option for presenting my bait delicately and accurately. However, I also set up a waggler rod and a bomb rod in case I needed to fish further out in the open water, or to reach the island to my right.

At 9am sharp the 'all in' was called and the match began. I baited with a single maggot and shipped out to my swim at 6 metres. I also catapulted in a small quantity of maggots and a couple of grains of corn around my float, to try to attract fish into the swim.

I didn't have too long to wait for something to happen. We had only been fishing for some 15 minutes before my float shot under and I lifted into a small roach of a couple of ounces in weight. Quickly unhooking it and placing it in my keepnet I re-baited and shipped back out, again also firing in some loose offerings around my float.

I was pleased to have caught this roach, albeit a little one, as catching your first fish in a match always settles the nerves a little and has you breathing a little more calmly.

Almost immediately the float went under again and I was into another small roach. This pattern repeated itself until I quite quickly had six small roach in my net, so I decided to switch baits to sweetcorn to see if I could target a better stamp of roach as I was sure I must have a shoal of them in front of me and a slightly larger bait would, hopefully, prevent the smaller fish from getting in first before the larger fish.

As expected, I had to wait a little longer for the next bite, but again it was a clear indication as the float slid under and

I lifted into what felt like a better fish. It was indeed another roach, but this time a bigger fish weighing about 10 ounces.

I was delighted that my match was going to plan and started to feel reasonably confident, because I could see that the first few anglers to my right and left were not catching. However, there were still another six or seven anglers that I couldn't see, so I had no idea how they were going. Therefore, I needed to press on and keep putting fish in the net.

I shipped back out with another single grain of corn on the hook, again loose feeding a few maggots and grains of corn around my float. Quite quickly I caught another roach of about 10 ounces. Then nothing happened for a while and I began to wonder if the roach shoal had moved away. If so, I hoped that perhaps something larger had moved into the swim and pushed the roach out.

Suddenly, the float tip shuddered slightly, although did not go under. I waited, with my heart pounding, resisting the urge to strike, to see if the bite would develop. Sure enough, the float shuddered again and this time also dipped slightly. It then started to move to the left and I counted to three before lifting the pole tip.

Immediately something powerful roared off, pulling the green elastic out of my pole tip. I could do nothing except apply some sideways pressure and hope that the fish would stop its run before the line broke. The elastic must have been almost at full stretch before, thankfully, the fish turned and started to slowly come back towards me. I gradually shipped my pole back until I only had my top kit and one section in my hand. The fish was by now just in front of me and I attempted to bring it to the surface by lifting the pole. As soon as I tried this, the fish lunged strongly downwards and I was forced to quickly lower the pole again to cushion against the lunge and protect the line from breaking. This happened another three or four times until, at last, the fish began to tire and I was able to bring it to the surface. It was a lovely tench of about 6lbs. As soon as I saw it my pulse rate went up again, as this was a dream fish in match terms and I desperately didn't want to lose it by making a hash of netting it (which I have been known to do!). Thankfully, the tench rolled over and I was able to coax it over the rim of the landing net before lifting it out of the water.

It was a super fish that I would have been ecstatic to catch at any time, but especially so in a match. I had a quick admire of my prize before slipping it into the keep net. Tench are beautiful fish, one of my favourites, with an olive green body and lovely red eyes. They are a strong fish with a large, paddle-like tail that they use to good effect. The tail on this one looked like a large paint brush, which explained why it had put up such a good fight.

By now I was quite pleased with how the match was going. It was expected that a weight of 8lbs – 10lbs would be enough to win, and I estimated that with the large tench and handful of roach I had about 8lbs in my net.

Then word came along the bank that another angler to my right, who I couldn't see, was also doing well. He had drawn a peg on the deeper water between the island and the western bank of the lake which was known to be a favourite area for the carp that were present, and he had decided to target these bigger fish.

If you have ever been match fishing you will know that the objective is to have the heaviest total weight of fish at the end of the match. Simply put, this can be achieved in one of two ways. You can either try to catch lots of smaller fish or you can sit it out and try to catch fewer, but larger, fish, depending on your assessment of the situation on the day and your knowledge of the venue.

Because of the peg that he had drawn, the other angler had opted to try the latter and catch one of the large carp that were known to be in the lake. He had been rewarded for this strategy by catching a superb common carp of 10lbs, which put him ahead of me in overall weight terms even though I had more fish.

I was now in a bit of a quandary. There was only about an hour left of the match and the tench had clearly moved out of my swim, as I was not getting any more bites, and I wasn't sure if the roach would return. Even if they did, I needed to catch probably another five or six decent roach to be sure of overtaking my competitor, assuming that he didn't catch any more fish himself, and I didn't think my swim had that potential.

So, after a few moments considering my options, I decided to try something different in a 'make or break' strategy to try to win the match. I plumbed around diagonally to my left until I found the old submerged causeway that in previous years had separated the two pools, where the water was shallower and where I was hoping that fish were patrolling along its length from one side of the lake to the other.

The water was definitely shallower here, only about 3ft deep at 10 metres out from the bank, so I reset my float to the correct depth so that I was fishing on the flat top of the old causeway, which appeared to be about 3ft wide at this point, and about two inches over depth to counter any tow in the water. I decided to stick with corn as bait, as I needed to catch larger fish if I was going to win the match.

For about 20 minutes nothing happened, then my float swirled around slightly and I guessed that some fish had moved into the area and had brushed against the line. Again, my heart was pounding with anticipation. Within minutes my float lifted ever so slightly in the water and I reasoned that perhaps a fish had picked up the bait and in doing so had relieved the float of some weight, causing it to rise. I lifted the end of my pole and felt the resistance of a fish.

Unlike the earlier tench which had stormed off after being hooked, this fish just circled around ponderously on the bottom of the lake and refused to come to the surface. Whilst I didn't have to worry about the line breaking from a strong run by the fish, it felt heavy so there was still a risk that the line would break, or the hook would pull out, if I was too hasty. I bided my time and slowly but surely drew the fish towards me. Applying steady pressure I was able to get it to the surface where it rolled on its side and revealed itself to be a huge bream!

With trembling hands I picked up my landing net and submerged the head of it in the water about 6ft out from the bank. I gradually drew the bream towards me, which was by now not putting up any fight at all, and once it was over the net I lifted, and the fish was mine.

I had never caught a big bream before and was trembling so much with excitement that I could barely hold the disgorger still enough to unhook the fish. However eventually I did manage to remove the hook and had a quick look at my catch before slipping it into the keep net. The bream certainly looked larger, and heavier, than the tench I had caught earlier but it was only after the match was over that it was weighed at 8lbs. Even now that fish is still my personal best bream.

The match finished soon after and Twizzle the bailiff, who had organised the match, came around with the scales to weigh everyone's fish. The other anglers gathered around as I took my keep net out of the water and murmured words of appreciation as I tipped the fish into the weighing sling, particularly when they saw the large tench and bream. The needle swung round and settled at just over 16lbs in total, which was enough to win the match and first prize of £20.

It was the first time I had won a match, and I was understandably delighted. The other anglers congratulated me on my win, even the chap who caught the big carp which, as it turned out, was the single largest fish caught that day. Certainly, if I had not caught that large bream towards the end of the match he would have won instead of me, but as we all knew each other he bore me no ill will – well not much anyway.

~~~~~~~~~~

Chapter 12 – Winter Chub at Buildwas

~~~~~~~~~~

Buildwas is a pretty village upstream of Ironbridge, a UNESCO-designated World Heritage site where the Industrial Revolution began and where the famous Iron Bridge is located, spanning the river at this point. The bridge was the first in the World to be made from iron and was cast locally at Coalbrookdale in the foundries of Abraham Darby III, the grandson of the first Abraham Darby. Darby started constructing the bridge in 1777, completing it in 1779. The techniques used in the construction were adapted from the well-established wood-working methods of the time, except that instead of wooden pegs holding the joints together, iron ones were used. The bridge is a masterpiece of construction for its time and still sits proudly, with excellent views upstream and downstream from its mid-way point, where a cast iron centrepiece announces its construction date.

As the river passes the village of Buildwas it embarks on a series of exuberant meanders, winding its way from side to side of the wide grassy valley which opens out at this point in the river's journey. The village perches on the hillside halfway up the eastern side of the valley, alongside the Wroxeter to Ironbridge Road which from this point generally follows the line of the river all the way to Ironbridge. The opposite (western) side of the valley along this stretch of the river is home to the occasional farmhouse and outbuildings, with small woodland coppices seemingly glued to the steeply sloping valley side.

Being halfway up the valley side means that Buildwas village and the road are safe from the autumn and winter flooding which frequently occurs on this section of the river. Once the river is free of its high-sided banks it easily spreads across the flat surrounding fields. The valley floor at this point is probably a half-a-mile wide and over the years I have seen it entirely covered in water on numerous occasions.

This stretch of the river is also blessed with a great diversity of wildlife, which a quiet walk along the riverbank will allow anyone to enjoy. Kingfishers abound, streaking upstream and downstream, and occasionally (if you are really lucky) alighting on a branch which overhangs the river from where they can peer down into the depths and seek out their breakfast, lunch or dinner. When they are perched like this it is hard not to be delighted by their vibrant and beautiful colouring – different shades of blue, sapphire and turquoise together with orange breast and patch behind the eye.

For the keen birdwatcher (of which I am one) this part of Shropshire offers a diverse range of habitats that support a myriad of bird life. The hedgerows that mark out the field boundaries provide cover and food for species such as house sparrows, hedge sparrows, greenfinches and yellowhammers; and the dense woodland trees clinging to the sides of the valley support large numbers of rooks, magpies, crows, buzzards and kestrels.

The river and its surrounding meadowlands, of course, provide a special habitat for many water loving birds and birds that feed on the insects that live close to the water. Species I have seen along this stretch of the river include canada geese, mute swans, goosander, mallard, swallows, house martins, swifts, and sand martins. The latter in particular are very numerous in summer, being summer visitors to the British Isles and being attracted to the high sandy banks along the river, in which they make their nest – a tunnel burrowed into the bank well above the water line. Throughout the summer it is possible to see these lovely small birds with their sandy brown plumage and white undersides swooping low over the water and the surrounding fields, collecting flying insects as they go, with which to feed their young. In some places, the sand martin colonies are so large that the riverbank resembles a Swiss cheese, due to the number of holes burrowed into it.

Speaking of the wildlife along this stretch of the river I even fancy that early one lovely soft summer morning I once saw an otter, although it spotted me before I spotted it and quickly dived from the bank into the water before I could get a really good look. However, it is known that otters are returning to this quiet part of the river as a result of improving water quality so I am as certain as I can be that it was indeed this beautiful, elusive creature.

This wide meandering stretch of the Severn at Buildwas has always been a favourite haunt of mine. Most days I can wander along for perhaps two or three miles and not see another living soul. The river here is wide and curvaceous with high banks, as it continues its journey through lush, grassy farmland which is mainly given over to the grazing of sheep and cows. These often-amusing animals are the angler's constant companion when fishing this stretch of the river. Cows in particular are inquisitive creatures and seem to come and watch me fish – perhaps they have a sense of humour too and enjoy a good laugh watching my sometimes vain attempts to catch the elusive residents of the river.

However, I recall one winter morning in late February when it was too cold even for the cows, who were busy being huddled up in what shelter they could find from the cold easterly breeze. With the Close Season fast approaching I was desperate to get in one last trip to the river before fishing pauses until that glorious day in June when the Coarse Season re-opens and anglers everywhere flock to riversides across the country to fish the first day of the new season.

In view of the cold wind, the low temperature of the water and the fact that the river was well up following days of rain in Wales, I was convinced that my only prospect of a fish lay in seeking out a chub, the one species which can usually be relied upon to feed in pretty much any conditions.

I parked in a lay-by near Buildwas village and, having unpacked my tackle from the car I set up my rod, a 10ft ledger rod, climbed over a gate into the field and set off towards the river. I was travelling light tackle-wise because I had a fair distance to walk to the river, and because I also wanted to walk up and down this stretch rather than staying in one spot, as I felt that a roving approach would present my best chance of catching a fish. It would also help me to keep (reasonably) warm on this cold morning. Therefore, in addition to my rod I only had my landing net, rucksack for bait and bits of tackle, and a small folding stool.

As I walked across the fields that sloped down from the road to the river my fingers were already becoming numb from the wind. I was wearing fingerless neoprene gloves so most of my hands were warm, but the exposed parts were rapidly losing their sense of feeling. The sky overhead was grey but sustained rain was unlikely as the night had been cold with a sharp frost. On the opposite side of the valley the tall trees clinging to the steeper slopes were bare of any foliage, their branches seemingly like bony fingers waving in the brisk breeze, beckoning me to the riverside. The lack of foliage also made it easy to see the rooks who had a rookery there starting to build their nests, their "kaw" or "kaaa" voices ringing across the valley, so evocative of this time of year.

As I walked along I could also see a cock pheasant crossing my path some way ahead of me, his fiery copper-red and chestnut-brown plumage, bottle-green head and distinctive red wattle clearly visible in the clear cold air. The author BB refers to the pheasant as "the Chinaman" in his wonderful book "The Little Grey Men", and it is easy to see why, as the colouring and markings of the bird are quite oriental (the bird, of course, being native of Asia and introduced into much of Europe by the Romans).

As I walked upstream along the stretch I intended to fish, which was about a mile or so in length, I looked down the steep grassy bank to the well-coloured river some six feet below. As I regularly fished this section in the summer and autumn I knew where the river undercut the banks, and where there were now submerged bushes, and these were the places I felt could possibly hold a chub or two. The river was pushing through quite quickly and it was likely that the fish would seek shelter from the current either behind a submerged bush or in an undercut section of the bank, popping out from time to time to intercept a passing morsel or two.

I eventually settled on a spot to start fishing from where the river ran down over a set of rapids then turned at an angle of approximately 90 degrees to the left (as I looked upstream) causing the bank under which I was now stood to become undercut as the current continuously eroded the soil there. The bank side also contained a number of thick bushes which were normally well above the water line, but which now trailed their branches into the river.

My plan was to cast upstream and let the bait come back towards me down the rapids, allowing the current to take the bait to where I hoped a hungry chub was waiting in the shelter of the undercut bank, out of the main flow of the river. As mentioned earlier, I had tackled up at my car where there was some protection from the cold wind, and was using a 10ft ledger rod, matched to a fixed spool reel carrying 6lb breaking strain line. I had a simple link ledger made up of four swan shots on a loop of line which was allowed to run freely up and down the mainline, but stopped approximately 12 inches above the number 10 hook by another swan shot. The beauty of this setup was that I could add or remove shot from the link as water conditions dictated. I wanted to get the bait well down in the water but not anchor it there, instead allowing it to trundle along in the current as naturally as possible. Bait was a large lump of luncheon meat, as chub love luncheon meat. In fact, at different times of the year they love pretty much any bait that an angler might use to fish for them, including worms, sweetcorn, maggots, cheese paste, bread and even large baits such as slugs.

I crept down the high bank a little way, so as to keep below the skyline, but being very careful not to tread heavily for fear of alerting the fish which could be just under my feet, in the undercut section of the bank. Careless footsteps at this stage could ruin the whole plan by spooking whatever fish might be there.

I opened the bail arm of the reel and cast upstream into the rapids. The bait landed nicely about three feet in from the bank and started to come back down the river towards me in the current. I closed the bail arm of the reel and started to take up some of the slack line when suddenly I realised that the line had somehow become tangled around the seat of the reel handle. I don't know if it was the lack of feeling in my fingers or simple clumsiness on my part which caused this but, whatever the reason, I clearly needed to free the line as quickly as possible.

However, before I could do this, matters took a different direction. The rod suddenly hooped over and with the line all tangled up around the reel handle everything became locked up, with the line singing in the breeze like a soprano. A chub, for I was sure it was a chub, had grabbed the lump of luncheon meat and set off for the cover of the partly submerged bushes (as chub are often want to do).

I couldn't create enough slack line to be able to unravel the tangle, nor could I open the bail arm to let out more line as everything was locked solid. I felt sure that at any moment the line would break, and I would have messed up my best chance for a fish that day.

Urgent action was obviously required and as, thankfully, the chub seemed content to remain motionless under the cover of the bush, I moved down the bank a little to try to reduce the distance between us and to take some of the pressure off the line. Then I realised that the part of the reel handle which the line was tangled around was the non-rotating seat of the handle, rather than the handle itself. Quickly, I unscrewed the handle completely and edged the line off the seat of the reel handle. Once free, the loop of line which was causing the lock up straightened out and I was back in business.

Screwing the reel handle back on I set about coaxing the chub out of the cover of the bush, where he had thankfully been sulking all the time I was trying to get my line untangled. Had he decided to set off downstream at any time then the line would surely have parted. Offering prayers of thanks, I applied sideways pressure and, gradually, the chub came around to my way of thinking and emerged from the bush. He now seemed to have simply given up the fight and came quite easily towards me. I slipped my landing net underneath him and with an internal whoop of delight brought him up onto the bank.

He was a fine fellow of about 3lbs with a dark back, lovely silvery flanks with the odd brassy touch, and a creamy white underside. His fins were perfect and a dark bluish grey in colour – a typical winter chub.

Even with my numb fingers he felt like a block of ice (perhaps that is why he didn't put up too much of a fight?) and I marvelled at how he was still feeding despite the cold-water temperature. However, as I said earlier, chub are probably the only river fish you can rely upon to take your bait in such cold conditions.

With the long walk along the river to the spot where I had decided to fish, and the episode of the chub and the tangled line, time had gone far too quickly, and the wind had picked up quite considerably. Being frozen to the bone and having attractive thoughts of a nice warm car I decided to call it a day. I had achieved what I had set out to do – catch a nice chub on a lovely stretch of the river before the Close Season came into force - so I walked back up the valley side to my car a happy fisherman, knowing that in approximately three months' time I would return to the river and once again fish for chub and barbel in that most lovely of settings.

~~~~~~~~~~

Chapter 13 – Autumn Carp in Australia

~~~~~~~~~~

As I mentioned earlier in this book, the current season of my life has me living overseas, in Australia.

Fishing-wise, Australia differs from England in that it has no close season - fishing is permitted all year round. Also, there is no separation into coarse or game fishing. Therefore, for example, a lake may hold trout and carp, and anglers are able to fish for both species at the same time, and at any time of the year.

The seasons in Australia are the opposite to the northern hemisphere so on this particular day I was going autumn fishing for carp, but in April (which would, of course, be spring in England).

The venue was Lake Burley Griffin, in Canberra – the capital city of Australia. The 664 hectare lake is the centrepiece of Canberra and was formed by damming the Molonglo River at the southern end of a wide flat valley surrounded by hills. Where the river ran there is a deep channel but otherwise the lake is relatively shallow for such a large body of water, at an average depth of 12ft.

Canberra is approximately halfway between Sydney and Melbourne. The story goes that both of these cities laid claim to be the capital, and as neither would give way the decision was made to create a new capital city midway between the two! In May 1911 a design competition for the new capital city was launched. The winner was an American architect called Walter Burley Griffin. He was greatly influenced by the City Beautiful and Garden City movements which dominated town planning in the late 19th and early 20th centuries. He also appreciated the importance of water in the landscape, as did the English landscape architect Lancelot Capability Brown, the designer of many wonderful English estate landscapes such as Chatsworth, Blenheim Palace, Highclere Castle and Weston Park. Burley Griffin therefore designed the city around a large lake, with the Government buildings on the south side and the city centre and central business district on the north side.

As I mentioned earlier, my intended quarry today were carp. European carp were introduced into Australia by European settlers, presumably as a potential food source, but are now classified as a pest, which is rather ironic considering the amount of money we pay to fish for carp in commercial fisheries in the UK. However, they are prolific in Australia where they have bred well in the warm waters and have displaced many of the indigenous species of fish. Perch were also introduced to Australia by European settlers and also abound in inland waters (they are known as Redfin in Australia – for obvious reasons if you know the colouring of a perch!).

As I set out from where we were staying, at 6am, a fiery orange glow beyond the hills to the east announced the forthcoming rising of the sun. However, at this point it was still dark enough for a silvery waxing crescent moon to be clearly visible in the cloudless pre-dawn sky.

Driving past the white coloured Old Parliament House building on the way to the lakeside, I could see on the extensive lawns linking the building and the lake numerous hot air balloons preparing for one of the regular balloon festivals that are held in Canberra. There must have been upwards of twenty-five balloons in various states of inflation, surrounded by hundreds of people who I presumed were either the balloon support teams or passengers eagerly looking forward to an early morning balloon ride over Canberra and its surrounds.

The weather had been cool overnight, down to about five degrees Celsius, but strong warm sunshine was forecast for the day, so I intended to fish in a wide shallow bay towards the western end of the lake where the water is quick to warm up once the sun rises, and the carp move into the shallows to feed.

I parked the car on the side of the road and unloaded my tackle before walking through the small grassy meadow that slopes down from the road to the lakeside, to a small gap in the lakeside vegetation which I had fished from before on a number of occasions.

As I set up my 13ft float rod I had a look around my peg, as I hadn't been there for a little while. To my right was a small copse of tall trees that hugged the bankside, whilst to my left was lower, more bushy, vegetation that pushed its branches and roots out into the lake. I knew from bitter experience that this was a favourite haunt of dashing carp, eager to snag the hapless angler.

Also from previous experience I knew that there was a small patch of clear gravelly bottom surrounded by weed beds, some three rod lengths out, where the carp usually fed, and it was my intention to present a grain of sweetcorn in this clear gravel patch.

I was using a clear insert waggler float because, whilst I had approximately 5ft of slightly coloured water to fish in, I didn't want to risk spooking the carp. Line was 6lb breaking strain due to the size of fish that I knew were in the lake, and also the proximity of the afore-mentioned snag to the left of where I was sitting. Bait was a single grain of sweetcorn on a size 16 hook.

I cast out and sank the rod tip under the surface of the water before sharply reeling in two or three turns of the handle to sink the line between the rod tip and the float which, being a waggler float, was fastened at the bottom only. Sinking the line is very important when waggler fishing to stop the line being towed by the surface current, wind or any surface debris that might get caught in it.

I placed the rear end of the rod handle on my side tray with the reel just forward of the side tray, sitting nicely under my right hand ready to strike into any bite. The forward section of the rod I placed on my rod rest with the tip just under the surface of the water, pointing directly towards the float so that I had direct contact with the float and bait in order to best set the hook on the strike. If there is too much slack line between the rod tip and the float it can impair the strike and lead to missed bites.

I sat down on my seat box and realised that it was a bit wobbly so stood up and turned around to adjust one of the back legs. Suddenly I heard a clattering noise and turned around to see my rod in the water, about 3ft out from the bank! For a second or two I just stood there, wondering how I was going to get it back, before grabbing my landing net with the idea of getting the net under the reel and pulling the rod towards me. However, before I could do this the rod slowly but surely started to make its way out into the lake, towed by what was obviously a large carp! I stood there helplessly as it proceeded across the surface of the lake before coming to a stop about 50 yards out from the bank. I guessed the fish had thrown the barbless hook (thank goodness for barbless hooks!) but the rod was now just sat there floating on the surface, clearly visible from where I was.

As it was the only rod I had bought with me that morning I had to think how I might retrieve it. I considered (briefly!) stripping off and going in after it but decided instead to be sensible and to sit it out and see if anyone came along in a boat who might help me. I knew from past experience that there are often early morning boaters, canoeists and paddleboarders on the lake so I sat down to wait for one to appear.

After about fifteen minutes sitting on my box, scanning the lake, I heard a motorboat engine in the still morning air, shortly followed by the said motorboat appearing from around the headland to my left, with a single male occupant, about 500 yards away across the lake. I madly waved my arms and shouted to the man, but he obviously did not hear me over the noise of the engine, and if he did see me he probably thought it was just some idiot doing early morning aerobic exercises that involved jumping up and down and waving one's arms about.

However, after about thirty minutes my luck changed as a man in a canoe appeared around the same headland to my left, only perhaps 250 yards out this time. Again I shouted and waved my arms and breathed a sigh of relief when I saw him look over towards me and change direction. As he got nearer I shouted to him to ask if he would mind helping me by retrieving my rod, which I pointed towards in the water. I saw him nod and wave his hand as he saw the rod on the surface and altered course to retrieve it. Having picked it out of the water and laid it across his canoe he came into the bank and passed the butt end towards me. Amazingly everything was completely intact, including the terminal tackle. I explained what had happened and thanked him profusely for his help. He smiled and said, "it must have been a big un" before steering back out into the lake and continuing on his way. As he went, I offered up a silent prayer of thanks for my kind helper - I never knew that angels came in canoes!

Apart from being somewhat wet, the rod and reel were still in perfect working order, so I settled down again to my fishing, determined this time not to take my eye off the rod for a split second.

By now the sun was up, and the clear blue sky and strong sunshine meant that the surface of the lake was a shimmering silver colour. My waggler float originally had an orange-coloured insert, but this would have been impossible to distinguish against the bright background so I had coloured it black using a permanent marker pen that I always carry in my tackle box, as this made it significantly easier to see.

I catapulted approximately six grains of sweetcorn as loose-feed around the float to attract and hold the fish in the swim. I like to only use small amounts of loose feed, so that any fish in the swim quickly finds the grain of corn with my hook in it. If you feed too much then there is a risk that the fish hoover up all the free offerings and move off, as they are no longer hungry, before getting to the hook bait. Even if they don't move off, it potentially can take them a lot longer to get around to the bait if they have to eat twenty or thirty grains before finding the grain of corn with the hook in it, so I find that feeding a small number of grains every five or ten minutes tends to result in more bites.

It was a stunning morning. There was no wind to speak of and the lake was flat calm. As a result, the city buildings and the poplar trees in their autumn golden finery on the far shore were reflected perfectly in the water. There were fish active everywhere, porpoising and even leaping clear of the water before splashing back with a big crash that sounded very loud in the quiet early morning air. If you have ever seen carp feeding on surface particles you will know that they usually come up to the surface then suck in their food from below; so leaping clear of the water is obviously not a feeding technique. I can only assume therefore that they do it for fun or perhaps as a way of trying to dislodge parasites from their bodies.

The hot air balloons that I had seen earlier by the Old Parliament House were now taking off and I could hear the roar of the burners in the quiet air. Suddenly they started to appear from behind the trees to my right, drifting low across the lake, a panoply of multi-coloured shapes and sizes, all startlingly bright in the clear early morning sky and perfectly reflected in the calm water. There were balloons named after a well-known Middle Eastern airline, one shaped like a can of lager, one promoting Canberra tourism, even one shaped like a dog! As they drifted across the lake the first balloon appeared to be struggling for height, and indeed was slowly descending towards the surface of the lake. In response the pilot opened up the burner and with a great roar, which sounded deafening in the quiet dawn, a huge jet of flame shot up into the balloon and it gradually started to rise, much to the relief (I am sure) of the six passengers in the large wicker basket slung beneath the balloon, who must have been wondering if they were soon going to be getting their feet wet. All the balloons slowly gained height and drifted off to the north-west, getting fainter and fainter until I couldn't see them any longer.

Including the little 'adventure' with my rod I had now been fishing for about an hour when, without any warning, the float suddenly dived under. I didn't need to strike, instead I simply lifted the rod tip to set the hook. Immediately the hooked fish took off across the lake like a steam train, peeling line off the spool at an alarming rate. I kept the rod tip low and to my right to keep pressure on the fish and, eventually, felt it slow down and turn back towards me.

I slowly but surely started to gain line back on the reel, keeping the rod tip low to the water. I have found that if you do this the fish will tend to stay near the surface of the water and you will have greater control over it, but if you lift the rod tip high it will immediately dive down, often with a strong surge that risks breaking the line or pulling the hook out. Therefore, it is best to keep the rod tip low until it is directly in front of you before raising the tip and quickly slipping the landing net under it as it breaks the surface.

The only problem was that this fish obviously hadn't read the rule book because it suddenly surged off, straight into the submerged tree branches to my left. Everything went solid and I was left wondering what I was going to do now. I tried lifting the rod tip but as I did so I could see branches lifting out of the water so it was obvious that the line was running underneath the branches to where the fish was.

Therefore, trying to lift it over the snags was clearly not going to work so I tried another ploy, easing off the pressure and giving the fish line in the hope that it would bolt back out into open water once it felt no resistance. Unfortunately it decided to sit there and sulk instead, so after maybe thirty seconds I decided to sink the rod tip low into the water to my right and began to apply steady sideways pressure. Amazingly, and with a sudden surge, the fish came out of the branches and back into open water.

Breathing a sigh of relief I steadily wound the fish in until I had it in front of me. I could see that it was a common carp of about 6lbs but, in my excitement (and impatience – a particular fault of mine), I lunged at it with the landing net and instead of getting the net under the fish I hit it in the flank. Immediately it panicked and bolted off, breaking the line at the hook knot.

Cursing myself for my stupidity, I refrained from throwing the rod and landing net in the lake in a juvenile fit of rage and instead sat down heavily on my seat box and took a few deep breaths (and counted to ten) before tying a new hook onto the line. As I did so I again reflected on the benefit of using barbless hooks, in that the hook would soon fall out of the fish's mouth and it would come to no harm, which is why I always prefer to use them. I re-cast and set the rod in the rod rest again, to await what I hoped would be another bite.

The wildlife on and around the lake is quite diverse. The bushes to my left were filled with fairy wrens, which are like a cross between a British wren and long-tailed tit, in that they have a long tail and are full of non-stop energy, constantly flitting from branch to branch in search of food and hardly ever settling for any length of time. The male fairy wren is brilliantly coloured with rich blue and black plumage above and on the throat, and a grey-white belly. As is common in Nature, the poor female has to be content with more drab colouring, in this case being mostly plain brown. The lake also has significant numbers of coots, moorhens and cormorants, which are similar in appearance to our British birds of the same name. Additionally, the lake is inhabited by the Australian water rat, which is very similar to our British water rat immortalised in Kenneth Grahame's hugely popular book "The Wind in the Willows". Like its British counterpart, the Australian water rat lives in burrows in the bankside of the lake and I have often seen them while fishing, sometimes swimming along the edge of the lake right at my feet (so long as I am quiet and still).

Perhaps it was the disturbance caused by the lost carp but some thirty minutes elapsed with no further indication of any bites. However, I was just watching a small perch swimming along the edge of the lake, right under my feet, when I noticed the float rise slightly before suddenly shooting under.

I lifted into the fish and, like its predecessor, it tore off across the lake at a rate of knots, taking perhaps 100m of line. I couldn't stop it as that would risk a break so I just kept sideways pressure on it, backwinding furiously to try to keep up with it. I prefer to backwind manually when fishing for large carp as I feel more in control then if I use the clutch, applying more pressure when I feel that the tackle will take it, and letting the fish run when it suddenly puts on a burst of speed, as carp often do.

The carp (for I was sure it was a carp by its power and speed) stopped its run and, instead, kited to the left, trying to get into the submerged branches further along the bank where the earlier fish had snagged me for a time. However, by keeping the rod tip low to the water and applying sideways pressure I was able to steer it away from the snags and keep it in open water. The problem was that it felt heavier than the earlier fish so I couldn't be too gung-ho with it, and every time I got it close to the bank it turned and tore back off across the lake, and I was powerless to stop it. Eventually, however, the length of the runs diminished each time and I felt sure that I was winning the battle.

By now my right arm was aching and I was having to also use my left hand on the rod, placing it about a foot above my reel hand to provide additional leverage. But the carp was also tiring. Finally, it came to the surface and rolled on its side. I slowly eased it towards me and over the submerged landing net, taking more care this time! I raised the net and it gave one last explosive splash as it realised it was netted.

I couldn't lift the net out of the water for fear of snapping the carbon fibre handle, so I pulled the handle towards and behind me until the net head was at my feet. I then lifted it out of the water, needing both hands as the fish felt very heavy.

I quickly unscrewed the net head from the handle and weighed my prize in the net. The scales showed 8lbs of pristine common carp. What was also amazing was how warm to the touch the fish was. The recent weeks of strong daytime sunshine had warmed the water tremendously and I later checked the water temperature to find out that it was 25 degrees celsius! No wonder the fish was so full of fight, and also why it felt like it had been poached in a pot of hot water! I paused for a minute to admire its beauty before slipping it back into its warm bath, where it quickly disappeared into the depths, none the worse for its adventure.

By this time the sun was high in the sky and extremely warm, and I reasoned that the carp would soon cease feeding until the evening when it would be a little cooler, so I packed up my gear, walked back across the little grassy meadow to the car and made my way back to our accommodation. As I did so I reflected that I was very blessed to be able to fish for such large and hard fighting carp in such beautiful surroundings, and amidst such wonderful wildlife. I had to admit though to a touch of sadness that it was not my beloved River Severn which, throughout my earlier life seasons, had been my companion and my joy. However, on a more positive note, I looked forward to returning to the river, its company, its wildlife and its fishing once again soon, perhaps in the next chapter of my life, to enjoy more 'Seasons on the Severn'.

~~~~~~~~~~

9 781803 694801